The Space and Practice of Reading

Mirroring worldwide debates on social class, literacy rates, and social change, this study explores the intersection between reading and social class in Singapore, one of the top scorers on the Programme for International Assessment (PISA) tests, and questions the rhetoric of social change that does not take into account local spaces and practices. This comparative study of reading practices in an elite school and a government school in Singapore draws on practice and spatial perspectives to provide critical insight into how taken-for-granted practices and spaces of reading can be in fact unacknowledged spaces of inequity. Acknowledging the role of social class in shaping reading education is a start to reconfiguring current practices and spaces for more effective and equitable reading practices. This book shows how using localised, contextualised approaches sensitive to the home, school, national and global contexts can lead to more targeted policy and practice transformation in the area of reading instruction and intervention.

Chapters in the book include:

- Becoming a Reader: Home-School Connections
- Singaporean Boys Constructing Global Literate Selves: School-Nation Connections
- Levelling the Reading Gap: Socio-Spatial Perspectives

The book will be relevant to literacy scholars and educators, library science researchers and sociologists interested in the intersection of class and literacy practices in the 21st century.

Chin Ee Loh is Assistant Professor at the National Institute of Education, Nanyang Technological University.

The Space and Practice of Reading
A Case Study of Reading and Social Class in Singapore

Chin Ee Loh

LONDON AND NEW YORK

First published 2017
by Routledge
2 Park Square, Milton Park, Abingdon, Oxon OX14 4RN

and by Routledge
711 Third Avenue, New York, NY 10017

Routledge is an imprint of the Taylor & Francis Group, an informa business

© 2017 Chin Ee Loh

The right of Chin Ee Loh to be identified as author of this work has been asserted by her in accordance with sections 77 and 78 of the Copyright, Designs and Patents Act 1988.

All rights reserved. No part of this book may be reprinted or reproduced or utilised in any form or by any electronic, mechanical, or other means, now known or hereafter invented, including photocopying and recording, or in any information storage or retrieval system, without permission in writing from the publishers.

Trademark notice: Product or corporate names may be trademarks or registered trademarks, and are used only for identification and explanation without intent to infringe.

British Library Cataloguing-in-Publication Data
A catalogue record for this book is available from the British Library

Library of Congress Cataloging-in-Publication Data
A catalog record for this book has been requested

ISBN: 978-1-138-91850-4 (hbk)
ISBN: 978-1-315-68845-9 (ebk)

Typeset in Galliard
by Apex CoVantage, LLC

Printed and bound in Great Britain by
TJ International Ltd, Padstow, Cornwall

This book is dedicated to my family – my husband, Mark Tay, and children, Tze Ern and Min Ern.

Contents

List of figures viii
List of tables ix
Acknowledgements x
Preface xii

1 Introduction: social class, cultural capital, and reading 1

2 *Becoming* a reader: home-school connections 25

3 Singaporean boys constructing global literate selves: school-nation connections 45

4 *Levelling* the reading gap: socio-spatial perspectives 66

5 Conclusion: the space and practice of reading 89

Appendix 105
References 106
Index 126

Figures

2.1	Invisible network of resources	29
4.1	Map of Tembusu Media Resource Library	76
4.2	Map of Ace Institution library, top level	78
4.3	Layout of tables at Tembusu	78
4.4	Tembusu careers' corner	79
4.5	Physical, social and affective comparison of Tembusu library and Ace library	80

Tables

1.1	Comparison of students' network of resources	19
2.1	Ace Institution boys' reading resources	30
2.2	Tembusu boys' reading resources	36
2.3	Sample responses for functional and aesthetic views towards reading	40
3.1	IBDP English A1 texts studied in 2006	53

Acknowledgements

My interest in practice theorists and social class began at the University at Albany, State University of New York, when I attended James Collins's course, ERGD711 *Literacy as Social Reproduction and Transformation* in the fall of 2007. I would like to thank him for inspiring me to get started on the path to exploring literacy as a complex practice to be understood in particular contexts of use and for the continuing conversations on my work snatched at conferences and rare visits back to the States. My dissertation supervisor, Jane Agee, guided me through my dissertation work with much patience and care. Arthur Applebee and Judith Langer were teachers and mentors who provided me with many opportunities to learn through observation, lessons and discussion in their classes and as a research assistant on the National Study of Writing Instruction project. Many thanks to Robert Bangert-Drowns for understanding the importance of collaboration and conversation and providing opportunities for students to share their work during the Albany Consortium for Research in Instructional Design and Theory (ACRI-DAT) forums. To my fellow researcher and course mates, Sedef Uzuner Smith and Anne Marie Bonafide, thank you for your encouragement and support.

I am also appreciative for my colleagues at the National Institute of Education (NIE), Nanyang Technological University, who believed in the value of my work and encouraged me to press on with the research and writing. Angelia Poon, Aaron Koh, and Richard Young (who was visiting from the University of Wisconsin–Madison from 2012 to 2013) were insistent that my work should be written up and confident that I would somehow manage to balance being both a good parent and researcher. Aaron Koh was instrumental in providing encouragement and invaluable feedback on my initial proposal for the book. Anneliese Kramer-Dahl, Phillip Towndrow and Rita Silver kindly read chapters of the book, and their comments helped improve the quality of my thinking and writing. Whatever weaknesses in the text remain my own.

The book is based on my dissertation work and a second study conducted with the funds obtained from a start-up grant at the NIE (SUG8/13 LCE). A subsequent start-up grant provided additional funds for further research for the completion of the book (SUG 23/14 LCE). I am grateful to Lubna Alsagoff, who was head of English Language and Literature at the time I was completing my dissertation as an Overseas Graduate Scholar from NIE, for supporting my work, and for the NIE grants that allowed me to follow up on my research. My able research assistants – Lim Wei Yi and Edward Cheong – made research for the second study and for the book much easier with their efficiency and passionate engagement in the study. Melissa Ho helped to proofread parts of the final manuscript at short notice. Many thanks to Christina Low and her team at Routledge for their patience and guidance.

I would also like to thank the editors for their permission to reproduce text from some of my earlier work. The articles are as follows:

1. Loh, C. E. (2012). Global and national imaginings: Deparochialising the IBDP English A1 curriculum. *Changing English, 19*(2), 221–235.
2. Loh, C. E. (2013). Singaporean boys constructing global literate selves through their reading practices in and out of school. *Anthropology and Education Quarterly, 44*(1), 38–57.
3. Loh, C. E. (2015) Building a reading culture in a Singapore school: Identifying spaces for change through a socio-spatial approach. *Changing English* 22(2), 209–221.
4. Loh, C. E. (2016). Levelling the reading gap: A socio-spatial study of school libraries and reading in Singapore. *Literacy, 50*(1), 3–13. doi: 10.1111/lit.12067

Although I am not able to name the schools that participated in the research, I would like to thank the administration, teachers and students who so generously shared their time and experiences with me over two periods of time from 2008 to 2014. According to an Organization for Economic Cooperation and Development (OECD, 2013) *Teaching and Learning International Survey* (TALIS), Singapore teachers work the most hours worldwide, so I am extremely grateful for their time. I am also thankful for the student-participants for their willingness to share their experiences of reading and for recommending me some good reads while I was conducting my research.

Preface

Personal Reflections

The research drawn on in this book is driven by my own personal interest as a reader and as an educator who has worked in different schooling contexts in Singapore. As a teacher, I taught across the educational strata, from high-achieving students in the Gifted Education Programme (GEP) to students in the Normal Technical (NT) stream, typically slated for vocation institutions, before my current post at the NIE in Singapore as a teacher-educator. As a GEP teacher in the early 2000s, I was provided with much opportunity for training and curriculum development that I felt would have been useful to teachers of other streams but which was then not always available. I enjoyed being a GEP teaching and working with my students but felt that it seemed unfair that such benefits should be limited to one group of students.

My concern with social class also emerged from my own family history. My paternal grandmother was the principal of a Chinese medium school, and my relatives on my father's side of the family generally did well academically and financially. On the other hand, on my maternal side, I observed how poverty led some of my cousins to academic under-achievement and lack of opportunities later in life. I also saw how parental or adult involvement contributed to success even when resources were less than optimal. The all-girls' school I attended had a fair mix of students from different walks of life. However, in church, I mainly interacted with students from middle-class and wealthier homes. Exposure to people from both extremes of the wealth and poverty spectrum opened my eyes to the different opportunities available to individuals within Singapore.

The interest in reading is, as such, professional, personal and political. In my professional capacity as a teacher and teacher-educator, I am interested in finding ways to help students learn to read, to want to read, and to read better. Personally, I have always been a voracious reader, and while my reading interests varied with age and season, I am convinced of the value and power of reading for enjoyment and for developing the individual as a lifelong learner. As a parent, I want to cultivate a more equitable Singapore for my children to grow up in. Even though I belong to the category of a middle-class parent, with insider knowledge of the educational system (Draelants, 2016) that could contribute to my children getting ahead of the educational and credential game, it is personally unconscionable for me as an educator not to attend to "other people's children" (Delpit, 1988) who may not have the same advantages as my own. The aim is not to accuse middle-class parents of securing undue advantages for children. Like many middle-class parents, I too struggle with what it means to provide the best for my child in a highly competitive, uncertain world (Reay, 2013). Rather, I seek to question how schooling can address the inherent inequality of meritocracy, which presupposes neutrality to race, religion or gender for the selection of the best but seldom acknowledges the different starting points of individuals. Ever the realistic optimist, I believe that the educational system can be changed for the better.

Qualitative research, for me, is what Eisner (1998) describes as a way of "seeing", of finding new ways to understand education for transformation. This book is an attempt to understand how students learn to read and about how their life circumstances and schooling may encourage the development of particular perspectives and competencies towards reading. It is not a book about what kinds of reading strategies work best (for good overviews, refer to Pressley & Allington, 2015; Samuels & Farstrup, 2011). Rather, educational policy and practice must be localised, contextualised and enacted in actual school contexts, and my aim is to provide insights for educators to rethink educational policies and practices, taking into account the kinds of students being taught and the contexts in which they are being taught. By examining everyday practices of reading through practice and spatial lenses, this book aims to identify and locate systemic structural inequities embedded in reading policies and the day-to-day operations of schools to provide genuine opportunities for all.

1 Introduction
Social class, cultural capital and reading

This book is about how understanding reading as a social practice, particularly a social practice that is infused with the micropolitics of power tied to issues of social class, provides a powerful lens through which to rethink the way educators formulate reading instruction and intervention. Through two ethnographically-inspired nested case studies of students reading, one in an elite all-boys' school and another in a co-educational government school, I examine how practice and spatial perspectives of reading can complicate our understanding of what it means to read and to be a reader. Essentially, the argument in this book is that macro-discourses of what it means to read are embedded in the policies and day-to-day practices of reading and that practice and spatial perspectives can reveal how they operate on a daily basis. Making visible the typically unnoticed structures that shape home, school and societal perspectives and practices of reading allows policy-makers and educators clearer vision with which to shape localised reading instruction and strategy for more effective and equitable learning.

Reading includes meaningful decoding and comprehension of print and online texts, fiction and non-fiction. The concept of reading has expanded in this multimodal age to include a wide variety of texts and media across various platforms, media and cultures (Jenkins et al., 2013; New London Group, 1996). Whereas the concept of reading in this study embraces the multiliteracies approach, the focus in the research discussed in this book is on traditional school literacies. Certainly, whereas digital technologies and worldwide communication have a wide impact on learning and literacies, Warshauer's (2007) reminder that "competence in traditional literacies is often a gateway to successful entry into the world of new literacies" (p. 43) is relevant in today's world.

My focus in this book is on reading and learning to read as a class practice, where individuals learn particular ways of reading and being a reader from their class positions and inclinations (Solsken, 1993). Firstly, economic resources ensure access to reading in terms of material resources such as books (Chiu & Chow, 2010; Smith, Constantino, & Krashen, 1997). Secondly, understanding reading as a class practice acknowledges that learning to read and identifying as a reader are about values, beliefs and attitudes that contribute to particular ways of thinking about self as a reader and in valuing and using reading in one's daily life (Moss, 2007; Solsken, 1993). What kinds of capital do students mobilise to convert their reading as cultural capital into school advantage? How are reading identities constructed? What kinds of reading identities are privileged in school? How do students from different classes access these kinds of reading identities? How do home practices influence students' learning to read at school?

To examine the issue of reading and social class, I draw on sociocultural, practice and spatial perspectives on reading. Rather than viewing reading or learning to be a reader as "natural" or "innate" to an individual, this book takes the perspective that reading is a socially situated activity that can only be understood in its contexts of use (Comber & Simpson, 2001; Gregory & Williams, 2000; Luke & Freebody, 1997b). Practice perspectives focus on the everyday practices of reading, attending to how individual beliefs, values, speech and action inscribed on the identity of individuals are the result of structural constraints and individual agency (Bourdieu, 1977, 1984; de Certeau, 1984). Finally, spatial perspectives focus on the relation between space and social relations and can reveal how spatial organisation in classrooms and schools can provide or prevent access to reading (Harvey, 2009; Loh, 2016; Massey, 2005).

Common across these three perspectives are the following:

- Reading as identity construction
- Interconnection between home and school practices
- Relation between macro- and micro-practices of reading
- Power as a controlling element, whether explicitly or implicitly addressed
- The importance of contextualising our understandings of reading in the local context and its relation to the global
- Understanding the day-to-day lived experiences of reading
- The dialectic between space and social relations
- The view of the student as an active agent
- Equitable education and social justice

This chapter is arranged as follows. In the first part, I explain why attending to social class and reading is important. Next, I provide an overview of the theoretical perspectives underpinning the book and explain how sociocultural, practice and spatial perspectives contribute to our understanding of reading, social class and learning. In contrast to cognitive perspectives on reading, attending to the ecology of reading through attention to the sociocultural, practice and spatial perspectives of reading highlight that the value accorded to different reading practices valued at home, at school or within a particular society only makes sense when understood as situated practices located in particular times, places and spaces (Collins & Blot, 2003). This is followed by an overview of Singapore and the education system to contextualise the discussion, followed by descriptions of the two case study schools. Finally, I end the chapter with an outline of the rest of the book.

Why social class?

Social class matters for thinking about educational policy and practice. Although individuals may have greater access to flows of media and migration in an interconnected, global world (Appadurai, 1996), there is also increasing income stratification between the very rich and the very poor across and within nations (Bauman, 1998; Lois, 2014; Piketty, 2014) in these changing contexts of "time-space compression" (Harvey, 2001) and "liquid modernity" (Bauman, 2000). In this "new work order" (Gee, Hull, & Lankshear, 1996), the highly educated and skilled, what Reich (1991) terms the "symbolic-analysts" tend to be disproportionately rewarded, even as low-wage earners find their relative income reduced. Analysing U.S. data, Reardon (2013) notes that the academic achievement gap between students from high-income and low-income families has consistently increased since the mid-1970s, in part because of the growing importance of education success to economic success and the ability of high-income parents to invest more heavily in all aspects in their children's education. Poverty, leading to reduced resources and early learning opportunity, contributes significantly to academic achievement gaps (Darling-Hammond, 2012). Within Singapore, income inequality has also risen significantly in the last decade (Bhaskaran et al., 2012; Lien Centre for Social Innovation, 2015). Ng (2013), pointing to Singapore's relatively large inequality gap reflected on Programme for International Assessment (PISA) scores, suggested that "while on average Singapore students outperform many students around the world, there appears to be less equity in learning opportunities and outcomes in Singapore than the international average" (p. 371).

Traditional markers of class include income, educational credentials, occupation, housing, and self-identification (E. S. Tan, 2004, 2015). Also, while class has been traditionally divided into upper, middle and lower classes, class boundaries and features shift with time. For example, in their analysis of the BBC's 2011 Great British Class Survey, Savage et al. (2013) identifies new categories, including an "elite" class, whose wealth separates them from the established middle class, and a "precariat" class, characterised by very low levels of economic, social and cultural capital – categories reflective of widening income inequalities worldwide (Piketty, 2014) and global societal changes (Apple, 2010; Weis & Dolby, 2012). Ball (2003) notes three kinds of operations on class: class theory, which attempts to define classes theoretically; class analysis, also known as social stratification, which is the attempt to establish and operationalise class categories for purposes of comparison; and class practices, which "incorporates a variety of work ranging from consumption research, work on identity, workplace studies and experiences of oppression, inequality and social reproduction" (p. 6). My focus in this book is on class practices in the area of reading as an identity, "a lifestyle and a set of perspectives on the social world and relationships in it" (Ball, 2003, p. 6), embodied in a person's values, beliefs and actions, including ways of reading and identifying as readers. Fundamentally, in this book, I am interested in understanding how class allows or restricts access to reading identities and resources and, in that way, possibly contributes to students' academic and economic mobility.

School as an institution is a key mediator of class and can reinforce individuals' class positions or transform individuals and societies by preventing or ensuring access to various capitals required for social mobility. Students from upper- and middle-class homes often have greater access to economic, social and cultural capital (Bourdieu, 1986) that allow them to achieve or maintain their class positions by contributing to the child's ability and inclination towards academic studies and achievement. Participation in high culture events such as attending concerts and visiting museums (DiMaggio, 1982; DiMaggio & Useem, 1978, 1980; Jaeger, 2009) and cultivating reading habits (Chiu & Chow, 2010; De Graaf, De Graaf, & Kraaykamp, 2000) are commonly cited examples of cultural capital available to students from upper- and middle-class homes. Other forms of cultural capital may include the level of parents' education and their ability to provide transportation, childcare arrangements and extracurricular activities (Lareau, 2003; Lareau & Horvat, 1999). More recently, investment in international education through enrolling children in international schools (Doherty, 2009; Lee, Wright, & Walker, 2016) or sending them to overseas universities (Nogueira, 2010; Waters, 2006; Windle & Nogueira, 2015) are ways to accumulate educational advantage in a global market. This new "parentocracy" where "a child's education is increasingly dependent upon the *wealth* and *wishes* of parents, rather than the *ability* and *efforts* of pupils" (Brown, 1990, p. 66, italics in original) contributes to increasing inequality with middle-class parents using all means possible to ensure their children get ahead in the economics and social class game.

Social class thus matters when thinking about educational effectiveness and equity. Yet, globally, educational policy tends to skirt away from difficult issues of social class and stratification, focusing instead on less politically-sensitive issues of school reform and teacher quality to improve educational equity within nations (Ball, 2003; Reay, 2006b; Weis & Dolby, 2012). However, focus on school reform and teacher quality without attention to social class and stratification neglects the fact that educational policy and practice is situated in actual economic, political and social contexts (Bartolome, 1994; Mahony & Hextall, 2000) and that meaningful reform needs to ensure equitable access for all students. Discussing the shifts in the labour market and the deliberate work of middle-class parents to influence educational policy and ensure benefits for their own children in England, Ball (2003) notes that the prioritisation of institutional factors to the exclusion of poverty and social class in educational debates on educational achievement and "failing schools" in fact masks the diversion of resources from the disadvantaged to the gifted and the able students, who tend to come from more advantaged homes. Moreover, existing policy and assessment serve middle-class purposes by in part labelling working-class students and their families as failures. This deficit mentality results in teachers demeaning their students' ability and influences curriculum and pedagogical approaches (Reay, 2006b). In the U.S., intensely-segregated schools with large concentrations of children in poverty tend to be overcrowded and lack materials, trained staff, and suitable course offerings in comparison to more affluent schools (Darling-Hammond, 2010; Oakes & Lipton, 2013). The language of choice, competition and performativity (Apple, 2010) thus hide the fact that the disadvantaged or marginalised may have fewer options than the rest or that schools dealing with high-poverty students require more investment to ensure educational quality and equity (Lupton, 2005).

Ultimately, social class perspectives are embedded in educational policy and in the everyday practices of policy-makers, principals, teachers, parents and students. Reay (2006b), writing in the UK, has argued for the need to bring to the fore of educational analysis and practice the "absent presence" (p. 209) of social class. She notes that despite widening access and participation to alleviate social class injustices, increasing stratification and a lack of understanding about how injustice operates have led to most educational changes disproportionately benefitting middle-class families and points to how the prevailing fallacy that schools and good teachers can make all the difference masks systemic inequities that contribute to students' low achievement and prevent fluid social mobility. A social justice perspective, which deliberately brings "the management of the excluded and marginalized to the core" (Thrupp & Tomlinson, 2005, p. 549) in the area of reading requires attending to those who are disadvantaged in accessing educational goods as a result of poverty.

Why reading?

Reading matters when examining educational equity because it is perceived as a basic skill that bootstraps other forms of learning (Cunningham & Stanovich, 1998). The Organization for Economic Cooperation and Development (OECD) report on the PISA (2009) results state the pragmatic necessity of learning to read in the following way:

> Reading proficiency is the key that allows students to build on the skill base they acquire at school and to go on to become lifelong learners. If young people leave formal education before they have learned how to learn, they will not be able to update their skills to meet the needs of a fast-changing and increasingly globalized labour market. Economic growth depends, to a large extent, on a workforce that is flexible and able to adapt to different needs. Countries that fail to ensure that disadvantaged students can escape from a cycle of low skills and low wages that are transmitted across generations not only pay a heavy human cost, but also significant costs in lost productivity and economic growth.
>
> (OECD, 2010b, p. 94)

In a globalised market of higher literacy demands and need for constant upgrading of skills for new markets and times, the ability to read and read well ensures an individual's ability to sustain learning and income. Beyond economic imperatives, reading can be a form of personal enjoyment (Rosenblatt, 1994; Sumara, 1998) and encourages civic participation (National Endowment for the Arts, 2007; Nussbaum, 1997). In *Releasing the Imagination*, Maxine Greene (1995) argues that the wide reading of literature is a way to explore other worlds and understand others who live in different worlds. This disposition of openness that can be cultivated through reading is highly desirable in a multicultural world of constant boundary and people crossing.

Reading matters because it is possible for school and societal efforts (through providing access and resources) to trump socioeconomic status when it comes to social mobility. Although poverty is linked to poor early reading achievement (Berliner, 2009; Buckingham, Beaman, & Wheldall, 2014; Neuman & Celano, 2001; Smith et al., 1997), reading engagement and social investment in reading can mediate students' reading performance (Cummins, 2015; OECD, 2010a; Sullivan & Brown, 2013). For example, De Graaf, De Graaf, and Kraaykamp (2000), in their study of parental cultural capital and educational attainment in the Netherlands, found that parental reading was effective in predicting school success, especially for children whose parents have low levels of education. As such, it is possible for community resources and education to contribute to the levelling of the reading gap between students from different social backgrounds. More specifically, *engaged* reading (otherwise known as independent reading or reading for pleasure) has been demonstrated to lead to greater reading and academic gains, leading to better comprehension ability (Samuels & Wu, 2001), greater vocabulary acquisition (Sullivan & Brown, 2013) and improved general knowledge (Cunningham & Stanovich, 1998).

Much of the work on reading has focused on the early and primary years, based on the assumption that early intervention makes the most difference. There needs to be more research on reading in the adolescent years (cf. Laurenson, McDermott, Sadleir, & Meade, 2015; Merga, 2015; Moje, Overby, Tysvaer, & Morris, 2008) as students do slip through the cracks in primary school, and secondary school students, particularly those transiting from the primary to secondary years, still require school support to encourage reading habits (Laurenson et al., 2015). Understanding what motivates adolescent reading can promote the building of their social selves and improve their academic outcomes (Moje et al., 2008). Within Singapore, there has been a strong emphasis on reading in the primary years, first with the Reading and English Acquisition Programme (REAP) beginning in 1985 (Khoo & Ng, 1985; Ng & Sullivan, 2001) and currently with Strategies for English Language Learning and Reading (STELLAR) (Ministry of Education, 2008) to encourage a love for reading and a strong foundation in the English language. However, school focus on reading at the secondary level tends to be uneven, with many teachers focusing extensively on reading comprehension skills in the examination-oriented culture of Singapore (Albright, Kramer-Dahl, & Kwek, 2008; Hogan, 2010; Kramer-Dahl, 2007; Loh & Liew, 2016). Reading programmes implemented at secondary school level tend to include accountability features such as reflections and book reviews, and actual time allocated for such programmes tends to be crowded out by more examination-oriented forms of reading instruction (Wolf & Bokhorst-Heng, 2008). This reflects the situation in other nations where concerns with improving reading scores has led to increased pressure on schools to adopt top-down methods and other reductionist approaches promising quick fixes or short-term success on high-stakes examinations (Alsup, 2015; Soler & Openshaw, 2006).

My aim in this book is thus to move away from technicist approaches to reading to provide a more complex view of the adolescent reader and to use social class as a lens through which to understand how to implement more effective and equitable reading instruction and create opportunities for greater learning for all students. Central to my study of reading is the idea that we need to examine reading from sociocultural perspectives that take into account the everyday practices of reading both in and out of school to better understand the contexts of reading and reading instruction. Drawing on critical practice and spatial perspectives bring power and space into the equation to provide insight into how the macro- and micro-politics of reading and learning are intertwined.

Sociocultural, practice and spatial perspectives

Learning to read: sociocultural perspectives and social class

Much sociocultural research has demonstrated that social class is embedded in the way we learn language, which includes different ways of reading and valuing reading. Studies from what has come to be known as the New Literacy Studies (NLS) tradition focus on situated, everyday practices of local literacies (Barton & Hamilton, 2000; Gee, 1996; Gregory & Williams, 2000; Heath, 1986; Street, 1984, 1993). In contrast to notions of an *autonomous* or universal, overarching literacy, Street (1984) proposed in his *ideological* model of literacy that there is not just one literacy but many local literacies that need to be understood in their sociocultural and historical contexts of use. Moreover, he debunked the idea of a neutral literacy, pointing out that literacy is an ideologically laden social construct that draws value from how it is used and valued within particular societies. The attention to the social and the local in NLS work forms a rich body of mostly ethnographic work that highlights the ecological complexity of literacy learning.

NLS studies have documented how rich experiences of reading comprise part of the language learning experiences that prepare students for school literacy practices. In Shirley Brice Heath's (1986) classic 10-year ethnographic study of working- and middle-class communities in the Piedmont Carolinas, she documents how the children from different backgrounds learn different "ways with words" at home that better prepare some for schools than others. For the middle-class children from Maintown, their exposure to reading begins at birth with books and references to books in everyday conversations and practices. Bedtime reading, particular ways of interacting with books and talking about books, having models of reading in the form of parents and older siblings reading for various purposes and in different ways are part and parcel of their everyday experience. Children learn what it means to be a reader and to identify themselves as readers. In contrast to the middle-class children, African-American working-class families of Trackton in her study do not "read as an activity unto itself" (p. 231). There are few reading materials at home, and there is no time or space assigned for reading. On the other hand, the white working-class families of Roadville accumulate print in the form of simple books and are expected to "recognize the power of print to instruct, inform, and entertain" (p. 227) but do not learn to extend these experiences of print to their daily lives. Drawing on the same data set in *What No Bedtime Story Means: Narrative Skills at Home and School*, Heath (2005) explains how the children from the three communities learn "different methods and degrees of taking from books", and as such respond differently to school requirements of learning. Maintown children adjust best to school learning as they have learnt to connect what they learn in books and in print to the environment around them. On the other hand, Roadville children have had less "exposure to the content of books and ways of learning from books", and Trackton children have had almost no exposure to books and ways of learning from them. Middle-class children thus gain what Neuman and Celano (2012a) call "information capital" (knowledge about the world and knowledge about ways to obtain information) as well as different ways of relating to books through their reading diet, habits and practices learnt *before* they even enter school. This knowledge and ways of reading and thinking predispose them to learn more effectively in school.

Learning to read is often embedded in the language learning approach of the family. In Annette Lareau's (2003) study of the "unequal childhoods" of middle-class and working-class families, she pointed to how the families taught their children to use language differently. Language features are a key feature in family interactions, and through these interactions, middle-class children acquire large vocabularies and dexterity at verbal interaction. This oral communication provides an advantage in learning to read and also teaches the students how to relate to adults through language, a skill valued in future institutional encounters (Demerath, 2009; Khan, 2012). These communicative skills, perceived as innate fluency and adroitness in the children's speech and writing, become part of the literate repertoire of the middle-class child. The attention to reading and to language often forms part of middle-class parents' "concerted cultivation" of their child's talents and habits, marked by parents' investment in time and activities designed to bring out the best in the child.

However, concerted cultivation requires intensive time, knowledge and effort. While working-class parents also desire the best for their children, the quality of the resources may differ because of parents' differential educational background and economic, social and cultural capital (Chin & Phillips, 2004; Compton-Lily, 2003; Neuman & Celano, 2012a). In Chin and Phillips's (2004) study on how families from different ethnic and social backgrounds assembled activities to occupy their children during the summer break, they found little difference in working- and middle-class parents' desire to help their children and cultivate their skills and talents. Rather, middle-class parents' access to a wide range of resources, including economic capital, the human capital to know how best to assess and improve their children's skills, the cultural capital to know how best to cultivate their children's talents, and the social capital to learn about and gain access to suitable programmes and activities contributed to their children's summer experiences and gain in learning. The differential home access – mediated by the child's own temperament and motivation – contributes to the gap between the summer experiences of working- and middle-class children in the States (Lareau, 1989, 2003). In the area of reading, middle-class parents' own reading habits and resources, or investment in expensive reading enrichment and tuition, can contribute to their children's optimal access to learning to read.

These ethnographic studies examining reading from sociocultural perspectives provide insight into how children from different homes learn different ways to use language that in turn contribute to how well they learn to "do" school (Heath, 1986; Hicks, 2002; Lareau, 2003; Solsken, 1993). These ways of "saying(writing)-doing-being-valuing-believing" (Gee, 1996, p. 127) become part of the child's identity and are "sedimented" (Pahl, 2008) as part of their personality and natural predispositions. Yet, it is clear that class-based attitudes and practices influence upbringing and students' propensity towards reading and language learning in general. Hicks's (2002) ethnographic case studies of the reading lives of Jake and Laurie, a working-class boy and girl, respectively, demonstrate how the acquisition of a reading identity for these working-class children requires complex negotiation of their home and school identities in their learning to read and write. Growing up in homes with different priorities, resources and models of literacy makes the connection to the literate identities prized at school more tenuous. Furthermore, as they grow older, the worlds of home and school may be further distanced, leading to greater disconnect with school-desired habits and ways of reading. These class-based ways of learning begin with early childhood through primary school (Moss, 2007; Solsken, 1993), and the effects continue to carry on to students' adolescent years, embedded in their embodied attitudes and perspectives towards books and reading.

Beyond home resources, community resources may benefit populations from different social classes differently. In Neuman and Celano (2012a; 2012b)'s ecologically oriented study observing adults' and children's behaviours at the two equally well-resourced public libraries in Philadelphia, they noted that middle-class children tended to have richer textual experiences despite their access to similar resources. They observed that adults spent an average of 47 minutes reading to their children in the predominantly middle-class suburban library, whereas children were left to wander on their own in the predominantly working-class library. Without adult supervision and guidance on how to use the library or to read, the children often engaged in a "flip and leave" approach to books where they would select a book but put it aside shortly as they were unable to read it on their own. The lack of a knowledgeable other to help with the book selection or to read to and with them made the library trips of working-class children less fruitful than the middle-class children's visits. Neuman and Celano argue that this "ecology of inequality" disadvantages students from poorer homes and suggests that it is not just physical resources such as a library, books, computers and Internet access but psychological resources such as "the parents and other adults who make the many pathways to reading and information-seeking meaningful and important to children early on" (p. 123) that are required to ensure equitable access to reading and learning.

The sociocultural approach taken by these studies demonstrates how social class has an influential role in students' access to books and reading and to different ways of reading that may prepare some students better for school-sanctioned ways of reading than others. However, Collins and Blot's (2003) critique of Heath's work and that of other NLS scholars is that they insufficiently address central questions of power in society and how power is implicated in everyday practices of literacy. Practices of reading and writing are "acts of self-making" (Collins & Blot, 2003, p. 97) as individuals identify themselves and are identified by others through their literacy practices. Possession of particular forms of literacies are infused with power significance in that they serve as status markers and provide for different educational and economic opportunities (Brandt, 2001). The ability to read, and to read particular kinds of texts, and in particular ways, are ingrained on the identities of individuals and can either enable or constrain an individual's ability to move within particular places and spaces. For the children of Maintown in Heath's (1986) study, the schooled ways of talking about books and relating to books that they have been socialised into at home is a form of power as they move with ease in school and in their conversations with teachers. On the other hand, the working-class children, socialised into different ways of relating to books, come to school less prepared and are disadvantaged when they are unable to display the kinds of reading behaviour expected by their teachers.

Practice perspectives: cultural capital, habitus and power in everyday practices

Working from practice perspectives can illuminate our understanding of how the micro-politics of structure and agency are played out in the everyday lived experiences of reading. Practice theorists such as Pierre Bourdieu (1977) and Michel de Certeau (1984) provide ways to think about how structure and agency work together in everyday lived experiences. Ahearn (2001) sums it up well: "The emphasis in practice theory is on the social influences on agency; human actions are central, but they are never considered in isolation from the social structures that shape them" (p. 117). Individual agency is constrained and enabled by the social structures, and individual actions also serve to reinforce or reconfigure the social structures themselves. Practice theorists take up the question of how social change is effected through the study of what Michel de Certeau calls "everyday practices", "ways of operating" or "doing things" (p. xi). The concept of practice highlights the micropolitics of power play, as it is lived through the experiences of the individual, and makes clear how power is embedded in social relations guided by structural constraints and enablers.

Discussing schooling and learning, Collins and Blot (2003) note that

> ... the school is one in a set of *institutions* which *regulate* ordinary people, a site for the practice of a new kind of power, in which establishing groups, precise measuring and recording, and the careful scheduling of bodily action are micro-techniques of a "disciplinary power" (pp. 170–228). This is a power which is neither central nor repressive in the usual sense ... instead it is pervasive and complex, insinuating itself into modern subjectivity, bringing the identities and physical characteristics within the purview of bureaucratic procedure.
>
> (pp. 73–74, *italics mine*)

Citing Foucault (1995), Collins and Blot point out that power is embedded in the very identities of individuals as they learn to construct themselves in relation to national and institutional discourses that shape their relations with self and to others. Whether students see themselves as competent readers and writers and how they judge themselves and others are bound up with official and situational discourses of literacy and learning. Within what Bartlett and Holland (2002) term the "figured worlds of literacy", individuals come to see themselves as literate and educated within "a culturally specific definition of desirable, valued forms of training, skills and knowledges (which may or may not coincide with formal schooling)" (p. 15). How people see (and rank) themselves and other people is dependent on culturally-situated contexts of what counts as reading and learning and often has a real impact on individual's social mobility and life chances. By attending to how power is inscribed on individual identities, and the connections among home, school and societal values towards reading, it is possible to better understand how social reproduction and transformation happen.

Bourdieu's concept of *habitus* provides a useful frame from which to understand the practice interplay between structure and agency, to understand "the experiential reality of free, purposeful, reasoning human actors who carry out their everyday actions practically, without full awareness of or conscious reflection on structure" (Swartz, 1997, p. 95). Habitus is "the durably installed generative principle of *regular improvisations* . . . a system of lasting and transposable dispositions which, integrating past experiences, functions at every moment as a matrix of perceptions, appreciations and actions" (1977, pp. 80, 95). The *habitus*, or an individual's life position, is a set of predispositions acquired by individuals through early upbringing. It is a "socialized subjectivity" (Bourdieu & Wacquant, 1992) where the collective meets the personal, and from this habitus, the individual is able to generate an infinite but bounded number of possible actions, thoughts and perceptions which then further influence individual dispositions. In the area of taste, habitus is manifested in "the capacity to produce classifiable practices and works, and the capacity to differentiate and appreciate these practices and products" (Bourdieu, 1984, p. 170). In other words, a person's predispositions towards particular lifestyles (such as a predisposition toward reading or particular kinds of books or ways of reading), often developed through primary socialisation in the home and early schooling, are so ingrained as to be seen as a part of the person's personality and 'natural' preferences. Chapter 2 extends on the concept of *habitus* to make explicit the home advantages that privileges middle-class students' acquisition of reading habits and practices.

Whereas Bourdieu's theory of practice has been criticised as static and unresponsive to change (Giroux, 1983), such critiques tend to be particularist readings of Bourdieu's work rather than on his research output as a body of work. Bourdieu himself explains that

> [h]abitus is not the fate that some people read into it. Being the product of history, it is an *open system of dispositions* that is constantly subjected to experiences, and therefore constantly affected by them in a way that either reinforces of modifies its structures. It is durable but not eternal!
> (Bourdieu & Wacquant, 1992, p. 133)

Habitus explains how individuals come to possess certain social, cultural and symbolic capital that are valued within a particular field of practice. Understanding how habitus is created thus opens up possibilities for disruptions and changes to modify dominant structures. Reproduction happens when these "common-sense" practices are taken for granted and replicated in everyday practice and policy. Paradoxically, it is only through the realistic acknowledgement of existing structures that we can begin to see spaces for transformation. The generative possibilities of Bourdieu's work and possibilities for change are evident in recent work on identity work (Holland, Lachicotte, Skinner, & Cain, 1998; Pahl, 2008), education and social class (Lareau, 2003; Reay, Crozier, & James, 2013).

The concept of habitus needs to be understood in relation to two other key concepts in Bourdieu's work, the concepts of *cultural capital* and *field*. Bourdieu himself does not explicitly pin down a definition of cultural capital. Lamont and Lareau's (1988) oft-cited definition of cultural capital as "institutionalized, i.e., widely shared, high status cultural signals (attitudes, preferences, formal knowledge, behaviors, goods and credentials) used for social and cultural exclusion . . ." (p. 156) captures the notion that cultural capital can be used as an inclusionary and exclusionary device for social interactions and for social mobility.

> Cultural capital is convertible, on certain conditions, into economic capital, and may be institutionalized in the form of educational qualifications. . ..
> Cultural capital, can exist in three forms: in the *embodied* state, i.e., in the form of long-lasting dispositions of the mind and body; in the *objectified* state, in the form of cultural goods (pictures, books, dictionaries, instruments, machines, etc.), which are the traces or realization of theories or critiques of these theories, problematics, etc.; and in the *institutionalized* state, a form of objectification which must be set apart, because, as will be seen in the case of educational qualifications, it confers entirely original properties on the cultural capital which it is presumed to guarantee.
> (Bourdieu, 1986, p. 47)

For middle-class children growing up in homes that value reading, cultural capital is available to them in the *objectified stage* in the form of resources (books, dictionaries, and e-readers) and in the *embodied state* in the form of particular dispositions towards reading. For example, the innocuous bedtime story routine teaches children to attend to books, converse about books, accept books as legitimate entertainment (Heath, 2005). These habits become part of a child's dispositions and are sedimented (Pahl, 2008) into their identities. The dispositions towards reading translate to an *institutionalised state* in the form of academic achievement when the students are able to utilise their rich home resources and dispositions towards school learning. The immersion in these environments is the students' habitus; within the habitus, they pick up knowledge, skills and dispositions that predispose them to reading and learning – skills and attitudes valued by the institution of school.

The field is the "structure of the social setting in which habitus operates" (Swartz, 1997, p. 115) and can constitute the school, the community, the nation and the academic disciplines within which an individual's cultural capital is given value or devalued. Individuals and groups struggle to gain dominance through acquisition of suitable capital to move up the ladder of social mobility, and positive reading habits that correlated to academic achievement serve as one form of cultural capital that is valued in the field of school and nation (Chiu & Chow, 2010; De Graaf et al., 2000; Jaeger, 2011). Where individual habitus is aligned with what is valued within the field, it is highly unlikely for individuals to question the common-sense organisation of the field. In the area of reading, those who are immersed in the culture of reading and its academic rewards are less likely to see how this advantage is accrued outside of their personality and hard work. The value they place on reading and their reading practices is a form of situated cultural capital (Lucero, 2010) that also can be converted into institutional certification, which can be converted to economic gain in the form of job opportunities and financial rewards. On the other hand, those who have not been socialised into these habits may see little value or find it more difficult to acquire these reading habits and practices and be excluded from the rewards related to such practices.

The concept of cultural capital makes it "possible to explain the unequal scholastic achievement of children originating from different social classes by relating academic success, i.e., the specific profits which children from different classes and class factions can obtain in the academic market, to the distribution of cultural capital between the classes and class factions" (Bourdieu, 1986, p. 243), whereas the concept of habitus is the explanatory device for how individuals come to possess certain social, cultural and symbolic capital that hold value within a particular field of practice. By focusing on the structure and competing discourses within which certain cultural capital is valued over others, and by recognising the influence of students' backgrounds through the concept of habitus within the field of the Singapore education system in a globalised world, the locus of change is shifted from the individual to the structure as a possible location for inequitable access to resources and opportunities. Chapter 3 explains how the acquisition of a global literacy serves as cultural capital for elite schoolboys and how national, institutional and personal habitus cohere to create a privileged space within which these boys learn to construct global literate identities valued within the national and global field.

The space of practice: reimagining alternative educational futures

Literacy research from spatial perspectives has gained traction in recent years. Research has focused on the space of the classroom (Hagood, 2004b; Sheehy, 2004), out-of-school contexts (Moje, 2004), online spaces (Leander & Lovvorn, 2006), curriculum spaces (Comber, 2016; Comber, Nixon, Ashmore, Loo, & Cook, 2006), the contrast between school and home/out-of-school contexts (Leander & Lovvorn, 2006; Nespor, 1997) and design of both physical and virtual learning spaces (Leander & Hollet, 2013). The turn to the spatial draws on the work of cultural geographers such as David Harvey (2009), Edward Soja (1989), Henri Lefebvre (1991) and Doreen Massey (2005). Space is significant in two ways: Firstly, by examining geographical distribution and access to literacy, spatial theories allow for a deliberate and systemic study of equitable access to resources for learning and open up alternative possibilities for transformation. Secondly, critical spatial thinking emphasises the socio-spatial dialectic, which is the notion that the social worlds we live in are shaped by space and vice versa. As such, it provides insight into how social relations within home and school are shaped by networks outside and within school (Nespor, 1997). It also foregrounds how the organisation of space may prioritise certain dominant discourses over others.

Critical spatial theories highlight the need to attend to equitable access and distribution of resources. For Harvey (2009), social practices and processes create and shape space. At the same time, space enables, constrains and alters social practices and processes. In *Social Justice and the City*, Harvey advocates an equitable geography that attends to how public goods such as housing and education should be organised in such a way as to be accessible to all members of the public, particularly those who are less well off. In education, critical awareness of space in urban policy requires an understanding of how policies and practices are influenced by dominant discourses of neoliberalism that reconfigure the relationships among parents, students, teachers, policy-makers and members of the public. The neoliberal discourse of choice and competition serves middle-class interests by favouring middle-class practices (Ball, 2003; Gulson, 2011; Reay et al., 2013). Not recognising the middle-class advantage and mind-set in educational policy creates a blind spot when it comes to understanding educational disadvantage for the poor. In this book, I suggest that through comparative studies of different schooling spaces, it is possible for educators to become aware of how their unquestioned occupation and use of space may actually be reinforcing inequitable practices (Massey, 2005; Soja, 1989). Zooming in on uses of space and social relations created through spatial organisation within each specific context allows educators to understand and evaluate whether reading policies and practices are effective and equitable.

Space shapes social relations within the space and vice versa (Lefebvre, 1991). Competing discourses shape the organisation of space and the lived experiences within a particular place. In Nespor's (1997) ethnographic study of Thurber Elementary in Roanoke, Virginia, she utilises the concept of circuits and fields to explain the "networks of practices that orient people within arenas of institutional life" (p. 25). Although the school is bounded within a particular physical place, the practices within school are directed and influenced by policies and practices, networks of relations and understandings within the nation, community and school. Focusing on space, particularly lived space, is a way to unearth the dominant discourses shaping practices in the field and to understand how our common-sense understanding of the world may be shaped by space. In Guitiérrez's (2008) work on literacy learning, she notes that the framework of "Third Space", which focuses on students' social ecology of learning, provides a "more productive framework and method of study that traces students' movement across their daily routines to understand what tools and resources are taken up or are available across the practices that give meaning to everyday life" (p.151).

Attending with spatial lenses to the day-to-day lived experiences of students within the bounded space of school or, in this case, the bounded space of the school library (to be discussed in Chapter 4) as a microcosm of the institution of school, reveals how reading is actually perceived and enacted within the school and allows for insight into how lived experiences are aligned or not to institutional design. By making visible the perception and uses of space, the aim is to open up alternative ways of understanding and responding to current lived space.

Rather than assuming the inevitability of a single dominant viewpoint, understanding that space is multiple, relational and open allows for the reimagination of how space can and should be used equitably to include different stakeholders, particularly those that are in the minority and marginalised, who have little chance and clout to represent themselves. The space within which practices operate is the field of practice, and struggles within the field of practice are essentially struggles to shift how space and social relations are perceived to jumpstart alternative ways of reimagining occupied and imagined space (Massey, 2005). It is a hopeful endeavour, grounded in the belief that each field "constitutes a potentially open space of play whose boundaries are *dynamic borders* which are the stake of struggles within the field itself" (Bourdieu & Wacquant, 1992, p. 104). The ideas in this book are underpinned by the notion that understanding historical and social practice within particular spaces and the macro-discourses that shape the micropolitics of everyday practice make possible the transformation of space and practice through the transformation of perspectives and practices. Whereas complete equality may be impossible in an imperfect world, schools can either serve as spaces for reproduction or for transformation (Anyon, 1980; Bourdieu, 1977; Robertson, 2010). Making visible the processes that compound existing inequalities allow policy-makers and educators to understand how assumptions about the poor and about society shape policies, practices and spaces, and envision new structures to support equitable learning.

The Singapore context: discourses of meritocracy, education and economic growth

Singapore provides an interesting site to situate an examination of social class and reading. Lauded internationally for its excellent education system and educational innovation by academics, governments and educators all over the world (Darling-Hammond, 2010; Hargreaves, 2003; OECD, 2011), criticism has been levelled at official educational policies and planning for their tendency to sideline socioeconomic status (SES) as a factor for school success (Gopinathan, 2007; Gopinathan & Abu Baker, 2013; J. Tan, 2010). Previously a British colony, Singapore is a multiracial state with a Chinese majority (74.3%) and a substantial percentage of Malays (13.3%), Indians (9.1%) and other ethnicities (3.2%) (Department of Statistics Singapore, 2015b). Given its lack of hinterland and resources, the Singapore's government emphasis has been on people as "its own prime asset" (Olds & Thrift, 2005) to maintain its competitiveness as a world-class city in a global economy. Education takes on a "manufacturing" dimension (Koh & Chong, 2014), with individuals perceived as human capital to be shaped according to the economic needs of the nation, in large part through a centralised and highly effective education system. Remarkable educational and economic achievement is part of the official Singapore's success story: The literacy rate has increased from 73% in 1965, the year of independence (Goh & Gopinathan, 2008), to 96.7% in 2015 (Department of Statistics Singapore, 2015a), and Singapore regularly tops international educational assessments such as PISA (Goy, 2015) and the Progress in International Reading Literacy Study (PIRLS) (International Association for the Evaluation of Educational Achievement, 2011). In 2012, Singapore was ranked the third-richest country on the Forbes list, with a gross domestic product (GDP) per capita of nearly $56,700, after Qatar and Luxembourg (Greenfield, 2012). The importance of education to maintaining Singapore's prosperity and comparative edge is evident from government investment in education. Expenditure in education increased by 40% from 7.5 billion in FY2007 to $10.5 billion in FY2012 and accounts for more than 20% of the government expenditure (Ministry of Education, 2013).

However, despite the success story of Singapore's educational system in moving Singapore from a third to first world economy in one lifetime, unequal opportunities for social mobility have in the last decade become a real concern in Singapore. In 2011, it was reported that the intergenerational income elasticity registered at a relatively high rate of 0.58% (Ho, 2011).[1] Moreover, Singapore's Gini-coefficient rate has been for some time above 0.4, the level UN-Habitat describes as the "international alert line for income inequality" (Lien Centre for Social Innovation, 2015, p. 10). Ambitious growth rates, tax policies to support corporate growth, and the competitive structure of meritocracy contribute to widening inequality and increasing stratification (Lien Centre for Social Innovation, 2015) amidst the effects of globalisation that have contributed to widening inequality. In the background paper for the *Singapore Perspectives 2012* conference, Bhaskaran et al. (2012) noted that a new social compact is needed to address the changing dimensions of globalisation and society to build a more equitable and inclusive Singapore.

The dominant discourse that underpins Singapore's educational policy is that of meritocracy and equality of opportunity, justified by Singapore's economic success. Emphasis on developing human capital through education has contributed to this meteoric rise, and the education system is built on the notion that meritocracy will ensure equal opportunities for all Singaporeans to aspire towards upward mobility. However, there is an inherent contradiction between egalitarianism and elitism in a meritocratic system that is designed to cultivate the best and brightest in the belief that there would be a trickle-down effect to society at large (K. P. Tan, 2008). In principle, meritocracy provides opportunity for all in society, regardless of race, religion, gender or class to advance in society. However, meritocracy masks the fact that there are real advantages and disadvantages that are distributed to various segments of society (McNamee & Miller, 2004). The ideology of meritocracy may in fact enforce the entrenchment of particular segments of society by focusing on the incentivising power of meritocracy to efficiently sort out citizens according to their innate talents and abilities while neglecting unequal starting points. When official educational policies and research sideline class and other forms of differences as irrelevant to educational change, they mask the reproductive powers of educational institutions and may reinforce class stratifications within society.

Underlying the discourse of meritocracy is the tenet of efficiency. The educational system in Singapore is tightly coupled with economic policies, with education deployed by the state as a primary instrument for retooling the productive capacity of its citizens and educational policies shifting rapidly in response to the pressures of economic competition (Sharpe & Gopinathan, 2002; Silver, Curdt-Christiansen, Wright, & Stinson, 2013). As such, educational policies seek to efficiently manage students' productive capacities by "sorting out" (J. Tan, 2010) citizens at the onset of their educational journey. A differentiated education system, beginning with streaming introduced in 1979 under the New Education Scheme (NES), allowed students to progress at a pace more suitable to their abilities. The implementation of the NES led to an overall improvement in academic results and a decline in primary and secondary school attrition rates and resulted in greater educational and economic efficiency. Later, attention was devoted to the cultivation of top students through the establishment of the Gifted Education Programme (GEP) in 1985. A test conducted at Primary 4, and through the Primary School Leaving Examination (PSLE), a national high-stakes examination taken by students at 12 years old, determined the top 1% of Singapore students, who were then streamed into special classes designed to encourage intellectual and academic rigour and innovation.

The Singapore education system continues to be highly differentiated with varied pathways built in to cater to the different abilities of students. For example, students doing the Integrated Programme (IP) in top schools are allowed skip the O-levels, a national high-stakes examination, to focus on creative and critical thinking instead of preparing for national examinations. Students may also be enrolled in special schools such as the Singapore Sports School (SSS) and the School of the Arts (SOTA) or apply to schools through the Direct Schools Admission (DSA) scheme, bypassing central grades-determined allocation by the Ministry of Education. Students on the lower tracks also have more options: Students who do well at their Singapore-Cambridge General Certificate Examination (GCE) N-level may bypass the GCE 'O' Level Examination and gain direct entry into the polytechnics and higher-diploma courses in the Institute of Technical Education (ITE). The wide array of educational opportunities ensures efficient allocation of manpower for Singapore to maintain its competitiveness in a global economy (Goh & Gopinathan, 2008; Gopinathan & Abu Baker, 2013). Although the educational system is recalibrating to encourage more social inclusiveness and less competition (e.g., by investing heavily in early childhood education (Chia, 2013; Early Childhood Development Agency, 2013) and removing stress and competition by refining the PSLE to put less emphasis on the numerical grade (Teng, 2016), the impact of these policies remain to be seen.

It seems that students' access to education in Singapore is increasingly determined by parents' education, occupation and ability to invest in various strategies to ensure educational mobility. E. S. Tan (2015) reported from the findings of the Social Stratification Survey 2011 in Singapore that university-educated fathers are more likely to have similarly-qualified children (63%) compared to their counterparts with secondary-level qualifications (37%), mirroring international research on the effect of parents' educational level on a child's social mobility (Chiu & Chow, 2010; Sullivan, Ketende, & Joshi, 2013). In another study on tuition in Singapore, it was found that parents with higher incomes spend more on tuition, partly because they have more disposable income and because they are willing to invest more to secure an educational edge for their children (Teng, 2015a). Finally, the Principal of Raffles Institution, one of the oldest and most prestigious schools in Singapore, admitted in the 2015 Founder's Day Speech that the school is a "middle-class" school. He stated in his speech that with wealthier families giving their children an edge through tuition and enrichment, the PSLE, a national examination for streaming, was no longer a "level playing field" that allowed students from different socioeconomic backgrounds to enter the elite school (Teng, 2015b). As such, it is necessary to consider issues of social class in re-evaluating whether our social and educational policies are both effective *and* equitable (Lien Centre for Social Innovation, 2015; Mathews, 2016; I. Y. H. Ng, 2014). Examining approaches towards reading instruction in Singapore secondary schools is one way to rethink how current approaches to education can benefit from the acknowledgement that social class considerations matter in education.

The case studies: Ace Institution and Tembusu Secondary

Drawing comparatively on two case studies of reading in two Singapore secondary schools, one an elite all-boys' school and another a government co-educational school, the book explores the different reading practices of students in their home and school contexts to identify the diverse and differentiated ways that students learn to read and regard reading. The contrasting study of good readers from well-resourced backgrounds with a more varied group of readers, including students from low-income backgrounds, allows for insight into how students learn to read and how resources may contribute (visibly and in less obvious ways) to the construction of a reader identity. The book does not aim to give a comprehensive account of both studies; rather, the book draws selectively on the wealth of data collected in both studies to examine how readers from different backgrounds come to construct particular reading identities and practices and explore how policy and practice can benefit from understanding the connection between students' home backgrounds, schooling and national discourses.

The case study schools need to be understood within Singapore's educational context. As SES is considered confidential by the Ministry of Education, I provide a comparison of Ace and Tembusu's students' SES through a snapshot of the reading network of students, using the case study students' profiles in Table 1.1 as an illustration. The table reveals that the case study students from Ace Institution tend to come from middle-class and well-resourced families and, as such, have greater access to print and reading since an early age. In comparison, Tembusu students come from a range of backgrounds, including working and low-income backgrounds, and have more varied exposure to print and reading resources.

Table 1.1 Comparison of students' network of resources

Name	School/Track	Gender/Ethnicity/SES*	Family as Resource	Friends as Resource	Schools (Primary) as Resource	Libraries as Resource	Bookstores as Resource	Other Media as Resource
Joshua	Ace, Gifted	Male/Chinese/Upper Middle	★★★ Mother used to bring him and siblings to library regularly; read to them; books at home.	★★★ Discusses books with good friend Robert.	★★ Reading programme in primary school. Reading list provided.	★★★ Mother used to bring him to library with siblings; still visits regularly.	★★ Purchases books from Kinokuniya bookstore.	★★ Plays, movies, YouTube broadcast of Broadway plays s.a. Wicked.
Sanjeev	Ace, Gifted	Male/Indian/Upper Middle	★★★ Not allowed to watch television; reads sister's books and books at parents' and aunt's recommendations.	★ Sometimes gets recommendations from friends.	★★ Reading programme in primary school. Reading list provided.	★ Reads magazines in school library; did not need to visit library since he is allowed to buy books.	★★★ Always allowed to buy books. Picked up books from airport bookstore when travelling, including Life of Pi and books by Haruki Marakumi.	★★ Movies s.a. Fight Club.
Edward	Tembusu, Express	Male/Chinese/Middle	★★ Has books at home; sees parents reading, mostly newspapers	★★ Discusses books with two school friends and a friend from another school.	★ Reading programme in primary school.	★★ Visits the public library every week before math tuition to read or borrow books.	★ Visits bookstore. Usually buys magazines and some fiction.	★ Watched and read The Hunger Games.

(Continued)

Table 1.1 (Continued)

Name	School/ Track	Gender/ Ethnicity/ SES*	Family as Resource	Friends as Resource	Schools (Primary) as Resource	Libraries as Resource	Bookstores as Resource	Other Media as Resource
Katherine	Tembusu, Normal Academic	Female/ Eurasian/ Middle	★★ Has shelves of books at home shared with parents and sisters; not allowed to watch TV when young, mother read on bus to her.	★★ Recommends and lends books to Maira and reads books recommended by other friends.	★★ Comes from all-girls' primary school with strong reading culture.	★ Seldom borrows books as parents allow her to buy books.	★★ Spends more than $50 each month on books.	★ Watches book-related movies e.g., *The Perks of Being a Wallflower*.
Yi Han	Tembusu, Normal Academic	Male/ Chinese/ Working	★ Has four books bought in primary school; does not see parents reading; home language is Mandarin.	–	★ Reading programme in primary school. Bought some books to read.	★ Has visited the public library but more as a once-off excursion.	★ Visits neighbourhood bookstore to buy textbooks.	–
Maira	Tembusu, Normal Academic	Female/ Malay/ Low	– Home language is Malay; has no books at home; does not see parents or four brothers reading.	Borrows books from Katherine.	Reading programme in primary school but did not read much.	–	Visits neighbourhood bookstore to buy textbooks.	Has watched *Narnia* and watched the movie on free-to-air TV.

The stars provide a comparison of the researcher's observations of students' access to these reading resources, drawn from survey data, interviews and focus groups, and where relevant, reading logs.

★ Periodically observed

★★ Regularly observed

A newspaper report that nearly 72% of Ace Institution students have at least one university-educated parent, in comparison to the 7% to 13% from neighbourhood schools (Ramesh, 2011), gives a good sense of the different starting points for students from these two schools.

Both studies take inspiration from "ethnographies of reading" (Boyarin, 1992), studies focusing on reading as a social practice and Neuman and Celano's (2012b) ecological approach mapping the availability of print in two neighbourhoods. Three broad research questions guide both studies:

1   What are the reading practices (both in and out of school) of students in an elite all-boys' school and a co-educational government school?
2   How do these students identify themselves as readers?
3   What kinds of resources do they have for developing their reading identities?

The nested case studies, both conducted over a year in two different years, allowed me to "understand complex social phenomena" (Yin, 2003, p. 2). Comparisons help us to "see" better (Eisner, 1998); as such, this book takes a comparative approach by juxtaposing two nested case studies of two different kinds of schools and by juxtaposing students on different tracks within the same school. An overview of the data collection and analysis is provided in the appendix.

The first study: a study of good readers in an elite all-boys' school

Founded by British missionaries in 1886, it could be said that Ace Institution had always had its eye on the (English) world with its emphasis on the English language and culture, an asset even after Singapore gained independence as English was perceived as the language of business and eventually adopted as the language of education and business. With its long history of educational excellence, it was one of the first schools in Singapore chosen to become an Integrated Programme (IP) school, where academically-able, university-bound students are allowed to skip a national high-stakes examination, the GCE 'O' Level Examinations, and move on directly from secondary school to pre-tertiary education. In 2007, the school adopted the International Baccalaureate Diploma Programme (IBDP) as the selected route for students who qualified to skip the GCE 'O' Level Examinations and opted to do so. In line with the decision to adopt the IBDP for Years Five to Six (17–18 years of age), the secondary school curriculum (Years One–Four, 13–16 years of age) was revamped to align with the aims of the IBDP. Girls were admitted from Years Five to Six, but the school remained an elite all-boys school from Years One to Four.

In *The State Nobility*, Bourdieu (1989), writing about elite schools in France, explains how the "training grounds" of elite schools contribute to the construction of a sense of distinction in comparison with the common others. Similarly, in the U.S. context, Khan (2012) speaks of how the elite students at St. Paul's Academy learn "ways of knowing" that marked them as distinct from others and led them to believe themselves to be exceptional from the rest. The confidence with which Ace Institution boys carry themselves is a source of pride for teachers and alumni.

Michael, one of the case study participants, informed me during an interview that he could have gone to any school in Singapore but chose Ace Institution because of the "confidence that Ace boys have".

Ace Institution positioned itself as a school that prepared its students to be suitably literate in a fast-globalising world, and its aim towards internationalism was evident in the school's IBDP's motto – "Scholar, Leader and Global Citizen". School curricula, school-organised activities and overseas exposure trips were all geared towards providing the environment for students to learn to become global citizens. In the hypercompetitive educational climate of Singapore, Ace Institution students were given many opportunities to perform academically and in their extracurricular activities. Trophies for sporting, artistic and uniformed groups lined the main foyer and the principal's office and contributed to a sense of history and excellence. Most Ace students expected to go to the university, and the school boasted of a large number of Ivy League entrants and students who had been awarded prestigious scholarships. The alumni boasted of successful professionals, businessmen, politicians, thespians, and large numbers of the students were proud to admit that they were second- or third-generation "Ace-sians". Ace Institution students more often than not display a sense of assuredness (Forbes & Lingard, 2013) in the way they related to others and with regard to their possible futures. A long-time teacher at the school described the Ace Institution boy to me as "confident, sometimes to the extent of being cocky" and suggested that "part of the confidence comes from speaking and writing well".

In my interviews and informal conversations with school staff, alumni, recent graduates and students, there was a strong sense of loyalty to the school's superior "brand" (Demerath, 2009) of education, which included being fluent in English (both spoken and written), having self-confidence and having a strong arts and sporting culture. Most boys in Ace Institution come from homes where English is the language of home communication, and the emphasis on literary study there marks the elite school boy out from other schools where there may be more functional approaches towards English language learning. The ability to read and write well serve as decontextualised skills relevant for English-speaking markets, and the acquisition of the knowledge of literary texts was a form of cultural capital (Guillory, 1993) to position Ace-sians as well-read and cultured. Beyond the original British influence, continued government emphasis on English as a global language of business meant that the school's focus on English continued to be valued and relevant. In a national context where literature was perceived as difficult and limited to the elite fluent in English (Poon, 2007), the study of literature had symbolic value in marking the boys as belonging to an elite class where self-confidence and English fluency were their birthright.

The second study: a study of the reading practices of students in a co-educational government school

Tembusu Secondary School, a co-educational Singapore secondary school, is a typical government school in that it captured most of its students from the district and had a fair range of students from lower SES to middle SES families.

Approximately 40% of the students come from English-speaking homes, and the rest of the students come from homes where their mother tongue such as Chinese or Malay is the dominant language used. The school had a dual-track programme for students aiming to sit for the national high-stakes examination, the Singapore-Cambridge GCE 'O' Level Examinations, prior to their tertiary education. Students in the Express course take four years to prepare for the O-level examinations, whereas students in the Normal Academic (NA) course take five years to prepare. Another track, the Normal Technical (NT) track, prepares students for vocational training. The school's students range from high-achieving students who aspire to professional occupations and students who aim for vocational training after secondary school.

Historically, the relatively young school, founded in 2004, did not begin with emphasis on a reading culture. In 2010, the principal newly appointed to the school pledged to raise the academic scores of the students and enlisted the help of her newly-appointed head of department (HOD) of English to set up a reading programme. An Extensive Reading Programme (ERP) was instituted across all levels, with a compulsory 20-minute reading period set aside each week for students to read allocated texts. The school spent more than $50,000 donated from a charitable foundation purchasing books to ensure that all students had access to both fiction and non-fiction. Books such as *Charlotte's Web* (White, 2004), *The Hunger Games* (Collins, 2010) and *Tuesdays with Morrie* (Albom, 2002) were rotated on six-weekly basis, and a structured reflection was due at the end of each reading cycle. Students were allotted 20 minutes every Monday morning for reading their English books, and teachers were encouraged to show a good example by reading as well. However, the HOD noted that few of the teachers showed a good example, instead using the time to police the students or complete administrative tasks.

In addition to the reading programme, every Monday was dedicated to the reading and discussion of articles from the *Straits Times*, a daily newspaper. Other initiatives designed to cultivate a reading culture included inviting writers into school for assembly talks and partnering with the National Library Board (NLB) to introduce new books and run workshops for students under its READ@School programme. The English department also actively encouraged the use of Standard English over local culturally inflected varieties of English. This emphasis on Standard English is in line with MOE's official English language curriculum requires that students learn to "[s]peak, write and represent in internationally acceptable English (Standard English) that is grammatical, fluent, mutually intelligible and appropriate for different purposes, audiences, contexts and cultures" (Ministry of Education, 2010, p. 10). Yet, the linguistic and cultural reality at Tembusu Secondary is that many of its students come from non-English speaking homes, with an increasing number of foreign students from non-English speaking countries such as China and Thailand adding to the struggles of English teachers (Loh & Liew, 2016). Overall, the HOD shared that there had been perceived improvement in students' academic results in the last few years, even though teachers still struggle to get students to read more and to write and speak well.

The focus of the book

Chapters 2 to 4 can be read as stand-alone but interconnected chapters. The running theme across the chapters is the need to make visible the invisible structures of class through attention to the social networks that support the development of a reading identity that is aligned with school-desired ways of reading in Chapter 2; the kinds of knowledge, skills and dispositions that are cultivated in Chapter 3; and the spaces of reading within schools in Chapter 4. Chapter 2 focuses on reading as a social practice to trace how reading identities are tied to social networks and resources surrounding individual students. Drawing on Bourdieu's concept of habitus, I elaborate on how an *invisible network of resources* shapes the probable development of reading identities of individual students. I locate the discussion of the reading identities at the intersection of gender and class to demonstrate how they contribute to different definitions of and responses to reading that may translate to real advantages in school learning. Chapter 3 traces how the Ace Institution boys acquire *global literate identities* through their home, peer and school practices and link the development of these global literate identities to the policy discourses that encourage these flexible identities for top students. These boys develop a flexible and tactical literacy that allows them to easily traverse the worlds of school, nation and world, but I question if the acquisitions of particular ways of reading should be limited to particular students. Chapter 4 examines the space of the school library as a central but neglected space for cultivating reading identities and practices, arguing that examining learning spaces through spatial lenses highlights how school design, organisation and programmes may in reality support or undermine the pedagogical intent of the school. Comparative analyses of the school libraries at the two research sites provide room to understand how space, literacy and equity are connected. Chapter 5 concludes with considerations of the implications of the findings for research, policy and practice, arguing for attentiveness to practice and space in rethinking reading policy and instruction.

Note

1 Intergenerational income mobility refers to the extent to which income levels are able to change across generations. Where there is complete intergenerational mobility (intergenerational mobility is equal to zero), there is no relationship between family background and the adult income outcomes of children. Intergenerational income elasticity is equal to 1 if there is no intergenerational mobility at all (The Conference Board of Canada, 2012).

2 *Becoming* a reader
Home-school connections

Contrary to the notion that readers are born rather than made, this chapter sets out to explain how the development of a reading identity is supported by an invisible social network and resources, often unacknowledged. In the first part of this chapter, I draw on the data from Ace Institution to illustrate how a student is more likely to *become* a good reader when provided with particular resources and support for developing a reading identity. In the second half, I contrast the reading identities and practices of the low-achieving boys from Tembusu Secondary with the good readers from Ace Institution to illustrate how the lack or abundance of these resources and support contributes to the likelihood of developing a reading identity. I locate our understanding of reading at the intersection of social class and gender to refine our understanding of students' identification as readers and non-readers and their reading practices in relation to their identification.

Individuals are socialised into reading practices that become part of our identities as individuals and reading persons (Hicks, 2002). Through daily interaction with and observation of adults in the community, children learn different ways of reading, writing, talking and valuing language as part of their "identity kit" (Gee, 1996, p. 127). They come to value reading (or not) and acquire particular reading preferences and practices, including gender and class perceptions and practices (Cherland, 1994; Moss, 2007; Twomey, 2007). In this chapter, I make visible the various resources that make the acquisition of a reading identity more of a probability than a possibility through the concept of the *invisible network of resources*. By making visible the material and social resources available to students from birth through adolescent years, I highlight how the development of a reading identity starts from early childhood, through immersion in print- and experience-rich homes. Studies have demonstrated that students immersed in print- and experience-rich homes pick up literacy practices, including reading and ways of reading more quickly and competently, and that students from middle-class families tend to have greater access to these resources (Heath, 1986; Lareau, 1989, 2003). However, reading instruction and intervention tend to neglect the sociocultural and historical factors that contribute to reading under-achievement (Bartolome, 1994; Delpit, 1988). Understanding why and how students identify as readers, or not, takes into account the individual histories that contribute to particular dispositions and attitudes and that in turn predispose certain students to reading as a valid leisure activity.

Constructing reading identities

Identity is seen here as a social construction, relational and subject to change (Gergen, 1994). Charles Taylor explains that the self is "essentially defined by the ways things have significance" (Taylor, 1989, p. 34) for an individual by what counts as meaningful and relevant to one's life. In that way, self-definition is a search for meaning, and individuals engage in activities that give meaning to their lives. Self-identity is also constructed in relation to others: "The full definition of someone's identity thus usually involves not only his stand on moral and spiritual values but also some reference to a defining community" (p. 36). Individuals see themselves as belonging to particular groups, or in opposition to other groups, as part of the process of self-definition (Gee, 1996, 2004).

For adolescents going through a defining period in the formation of one's identity (Erikson, 1968), the communities with which they identify shape their sense of self. Much youth research or study of "youthscapes" (Maira & Soep, 2005) have drawn on Anderson's (1991) concept of "imagined communities" to explore how youths construct new worlds in their media and social interaction with both global and local forces (e.g., Black, 2009; Fadzillah, 2005; Lam, 2006b; Maira, 2004; Schneider, 2005). Through their interaction with various semiotic forms, these youths form their multiple understandings of the world and construct their identities in relation to these understandings. Across these studies, it is also clear that youths' affinity with particular communities motivate their engagement in specific media forms.

Reading, and the kinds of texts read, serves as one of various ways for youths to understand themselves in relation to the world around them. Yet, classroom approaches to reading instruction with their emphasis on functional literacy often neglect the social element that drives students to want to read (cf. Ivey, 2014; Wilhelm, 2016). The importance of motivation in the reading lives of adolescents is demonstrated in Smith and Wilhelm's (2002) study of the reading lives of 49 diverse adolescent boys from three different schools in the United States. Drawing on Csikszentmihalyi's (1996) idea of "flow", or a state where people are completely engaged in an activity, they observe that "the boys spoke consistently of the importance of competence and control, the need for appropriate level of challenge, the desire for clear and immediate feedback, the enjoyment of losing themselves in the immediate experience, and the importance of the social" (p. 183). Student engagement in any activity, including reading, must be self-motivated by a clear view of the value of the activity, the possibility of individual growth over time and a social life that supports the activity.

Students who learn to *identify* as readers tend to want to read more, and as a result of reading more, become better readers. Hence, the importance of motivation as a key factor to consider in reading instruction and programmes (Francois, 2013, 2015; Gambrell, 2013). Understanding the relationship between reading and identity is also important because teachers make decisions about learning based on their perception of their students as readers (McCarthey & Moje, 2002). Rather than labelling students as "struggling" or "lazy" or "unwilling" readers, or wondering why imposed reading programmes (often implemented with much good intention) fail, examining whether students identify themselves as readers or not, and understanding why they identify themselves in particular ways, may help us to reconsider how to better help students engage with reading in specific school contexts. It may be that these students do not see reading as a valid option for self-construction because they have not been personally persuaded of its practical usefulness in their everyday lives (Moje, Overby, Tysvaer, & Morris, 2008). Looking at the actual practice of reading through social lenses can help educators to understand how to make reading meaningful to students and how to motivate them towards reading. Rather than seeing the student as a problem to be fixed, understanding the social practice of reading can provide insight into how the school structure and programmes can be changed to facilitate student transformation.

"Findings books" as everyday practice: making visible the invisible network of resources

In this section, I focus on the Ace Institution case studies to illustrate how a reading identity, taken for granted by the boys as part of their identity (values, beliefs and personality), is underscored by an *invisible network of resources* that enabled the acquisition of a reading identity. This concept draws on Bourdieu's notion of *habitus*, which is an individual's life position, or a set of dispositions acquired by individuals through early upbringing, and is embodied by being inscribed in "the body of the biological individual" (Reay, 2004, p. 233). The concept of habitus reminds us that individual worldviews and actions are shaped by the social and cultural networks, "sedimented" (Pahl, 2008) into individual identities through years of being immersed in particular environments, a form of "history turned into nature" (Bourdieu, 1977, p. 72). Engaging in reading as a preferred leisure activity, often seen as part of a student's personality and innate ability or predisposition, is in fact as much learnt through years of being immersed in particular home and school environments.

> Reading has come naturally to me since I was a kid. I read when I'm not doing something else.
> (Michael, Open-ended response, Survey, October 13, 2008)

In this quote, Michael describes himself as a habitual reader for whom reading is a default activity. The general ease with reading as a leisure activity and habit is reflected in the survey and in my interviews with the six case study boys at Ace Institution. The following group interview excerpt shows how reading was so

28 Becoming *a reader*

habitualised that "finding" and "picking up" books was regular practice for these boys.

Michael: Cliff recommended it to me. . . .. I wrote some freaking long commentary on my blog on it and everyone read it.
Roger: Really? I *picked* mine up in a bookshop.
Michael: I was like a freaking pioneer of *Life of Pi*.
Roger: I *found* it at the airport.
Sanjeev: I *found* it at home. My sister brought it home.
(Group Interview, February 6, 2009)

In this excerpt, the boys explained to me how they all came to have read *Life of Pi* (Martel, 2001) when they were Year Two. Although Michael had presumed that his blog entry had influenced other students to read the book, it was not the case. Roger explained that he bought the book for reading on the aeroplane on a family trip, and Sanjeev discovered the book at home. Books could be *found* at home because his family members were avid readers and often bought books that they could be left for the picking at home. What is striking in my conversations is how readily and fluently the boys could talk about books. For Michael, reading is so much a part of his identity that he bothered to broadcast significant readings online in his blog.

Their reading preferences and habits that may have contributed to their academic achievement were seen as "natural" rather than encouraged by an *invisible network of resources* (see Figure 2.1) of social networks and resources that made reading a probability rather than just a possibility. The invisible network of resources illustrates the various resources available (or not) to individuals to encourage the construction of a reading identity. The network is invisible insofar as these resources are seldom recognised as contributing to the development of a reading identity. Yet, a close study of the reading history and habits of the readers at Ace Institution for whom reading is a default leisure activity reveals how their habits of reading are encouraged by *intensive immersion* in reading and books from a young age (Loh, 2013b). The six nodes on the invisible network of resource (family, friends, school, bookstores, libraries and other media) in Figure 2.1 capture the different kinds of resources available to students for learning to become readers.

Like the middle-class children in Heath's (1986) study, these boys' parents valued reading and exposed them to print-rich environments from a young age, and these boys thus learnt ways with words that were conducive to the eventual acquisition of school literacies (see Table 2.1 for an evidence of reading in the six nodes). Joshua and Joel remembered weekly library visits, and Robert reminisced about his aunt reading to him during her visits. Michael remembered that there were "shelves of good books" at home, and Sanjeev shared that his parents did not think that watching television was suitable entertainment but instead encouraged reading by allowing him to buy as many books as he liked to read during his leisure time.

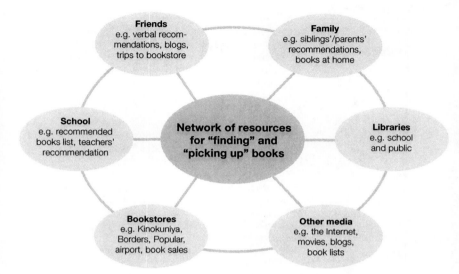

Figure 2.1 Invisible network of resources

As they grew older, the boys learnt to access books on their own through visits to the library, bookstores and online resources and gained more independence from parents and siblings in the kinds of books they read. Peer influence and school recommendations saw the boys reading Enid Blyton, Roald Dahl and J. K. Rowling's books as part of their regular diet, and their primary school curriculum ensured that they engaged with children's classics such as *Charlotte's Web* by E. B. White. By the time the boys reached secondary school, their reading diet and practices became more varied, although they still valued reading as a leisure activity: Jeremiah read manga on a regular basis, and Robert liked "Terry Pratchett and British humour", whereas Michael declared he read "anything" from classics to "chick lit" and Singapore literature when he could find the time. As I followed them from Secondary Two (14 years old) to Secondary Three (15 years old), I observed how their reading changed. Reflecting much research on adolescent reading habits (Maynard, Mackay, & Smyth, 2008; Merga, 2015), they read less as the commitments of school activities and high-stakes examinations took priority. However, they still saw themselves as readers and found time to read during school breaks and holidays. This identification as a reader is likely to contribute to their continual reading as they move into higher education. In Chapter 4, I discuss how the boys learn to read flexibly as part of the repertoire learnt from their wide reading.

This habit and practice of looking to books as entertainment was naturalised and seen as part of the boys' personality and preferences. However, as Bourdieu points out, "the ideology of natural taste owes its plausibility and efficacy to the

Table 2.1 Ace Institution boys' reading resources

No.	Reading Resources		Examples
1	Family	1	Joshua: Then, the whole family stashes our complete collection of *Tintin* comics and *Asterix* comics in there [bookshelf] too. Other than that, there's my dad's collection of *Peanuts* and my mom's collection of *Lat* comics (Email Reading Log, June 16, 2009)
		2	Robert: I was read to frequently and mostly from *Berenstein Bears* and *The Magic School Bus*. I don't think I ever needed any encouragement to read, although my parents were quite supportive and actually bought quite a few of the books I wanted (Email Reading Log, June 23, 2009).
2	Recommendations	1	Robert: It (*Four Loves*) was recommended to me by my brother because he read it, and it's quite a powerful book (Group Interview, February 3, 2009).
		2	Michael: My aunt has all the Jodi Piccoult books, so I just take them from her (Michael, Group Interview, February 16, 2009).
3	School	1	Roger: I remember quiet reading in school (Group Interview, January 16, 2009).
		2	Joshua: I liked primary school books. . . . *A Wrinkle in Time* I loved. *Frederick* was OK (Group Interview, February 3, 2009).
4	Bookstores	1	Michael: I just picked up the book (*Fifth Avenue*) because it was there (Borders) (Interview, March 27, 2009).
		2	Sanjeev: I go to the bookstore, usually Kinokuniya, and pick up something from the bestsellers' list. Usually I find something I like after four or five books (Email Reading Log, January 29, 2009).
5	Libraries	1	Joel: I mostly borrow books from the library (Interview, March 26, 2009).
		2	Joshua: I just found out there are two more books in the series (*Indian* series by Lynne Reid Banks), and I'll be borrowing them from the library (Email Reading Log, June 16, 2009).
6	Other media	1	Joel: I watch anime and read manga. It started with *Pokémon*, which I used to watch, and then I moved on to manga. They can be quite philosophical (Survey, October 13, 2008).
		2	Robert: I watched the movie (*Lord of the Rings*), and I saw the details, and it looked interesting, so I thought I'd try it (the book). . . . But *Lord of the Rings* is actually quite a good interpretation as far as it goes (Group Interview, May 26, 2009).

fact that, like all the ideological strategies generated in the everyday class struggle, it *naturalises* real differences, converting differences in the mode of acquisition of culture into differences of nature" (1984, p. 68). Thus, Michael declared himself to be someone for whom reading came "naturally" and for whom the practice of reading during his spare time was a default leisure activity, and Robert saw himself as "more of the stay-at-home type rather than go-out-cycling type" for whom reading was legitimate entertainment. Sanjeev "enjoyed reading" and could "devour two to three books in a week" during school vacations when he was less busy with school. Interestingly, five out of six boys mentioned airport bookstores as a location for picking up books, reflecting their lifestyle of constant travel and exposure to the world through both travel and books.

For the Ace students who had come from home and school backgrounds where reading was encouraged as a valued activity (both for leisure and as academic pursuit), the boys were not ashamed to identify as readers, even though they may have different reading preferences. Unlike the responses of the community in Cherland's (1994) study of Canadian sixth form girls' reading practices, the boys did not perceive reading to be a feminine activity. In addition, unlike studies suggesting that boys' reading was generally limited to non-fiction (Hall & Coles, 1997), these boys read fiction and read across various genres. The group interview with Michael (a national canoeist), Sanjeev (a school runner and prefectorial board member) and Roger (a violinist with the school symphonic orchestra) about reading *Life of Pi* showed how it was acceptable practice to read and to recommend readings, whether verbally or through blogging. That many of the boys in this class read widely and recommended readings to each other was borne out in the survey data collected from the class of 30 boys; even boys who did not identify themselves as readers could list at least four books read in the last six months, and many of them indicated that they sometimes selected books based on friends' recommendations.

Simpson (1996) suggests girls tend to engage in narrative texts that favour "discourses of feeling", whereas boys read less narratives but read more widely across genres and preferred "discourses of action". However, for the boys in the study, they did not see engaging in "discourses of feeling" as something that was contradictory to their boyhood. Michael reflects in his blog entry:

> Recently I have been noticing how beautiful life is. Perhaps it's due to the novel Cliff lent me entitled *Life of Pi* by Yann Martel. Although I've only read up till Chapter 17, but I can safely say that this book has been an intellectually challenging read yet one which could accompany you as you go through your lazy Sunday afternoon alone. It describes in length the wonders of this world as the protagonist "Piscine Molitor Patel" otherwise known as Pi Patel goes through different experiences as the son of a zookeeper and a believer of 3 religions: Hinduism, Islam and Christianity. Yann Martel has used the magic of words to allow me to understand this world better.
>
> (Blog Entry was shown during interview. Reproduced with consent.)

Michael reflects on the Booker prize-winning novel as an inspirational and thought-provoking book, expressing an emotional as well as intellectual response to the novel. Michael explained unabashedly to me that a good book "touched" him and that he was open to reading different kinds of books. The layered responses to a book also demonstrated Michael's flexible responses to books. He was able to enjoy the book as a "lazy Sunday afternoon" read while critically analysing the story and themes ("intellectually challenging read") and appreciating the language used ("magic of words").

On the other hand, although reading and sharing about one's readings were acceptable and even encouraged within this community of boys, boys reading "girl books" was not completely tolerated. Sanjeev's confession that he wanted to read Sophie Kinesella's *The Shopholics*, typically classified as chick lit, led to various reactions.

Sanjeev: I wanted to read the Sophie Kinesella –
Roger: –*The Shopholics* –
Sanjeev: But then my sis said it's so damn gay so I didn't buy it in the end.
Roger: My sister read the book. I saw the book. I wanted to throw it out. It looked so . . . dumb?
Sanjeev: Really? I thought it looked appealing.
Chin: (to Michael) Why do you read chick lit?
Michael: To understand the chicks better! [All laugh.] As in, it's nice. I think it's nice.
Roger: Don't you feel dumb reading it?
Michael: No, damn *shiok*[1] ah. Like, it's nice. I can relate to it.

(Group Interview, February 6, 2009)

During the group interview, the boys adopted different positions to reading "chick lit". For Michael, it was something he could relate to at that point in time (it was a phase, and he declared by the end of the study that he was no longer interested in chick lit) and was not afraid to admit to reading. Yet, in his introduction of himself during the survey, Michael was quick to portray himself as a jock ("I love sports . . .") who was also sensitive and open to reading different kinds of books (". . . and I'm a big fan of chick lit."). On the other hand, Roger vehemently opposed the reading of "dumb" books, a category to which "chick lit" belonged. Sanjeev, except for his sister's homophobic accusation that the book was "damn gay" might have read the book given its attractive cover and blurb. The varied responses to the reading of "chick lit" reminds us of the complex "tapestry of practices" (Ball, 2003, p. 76) within classed choices, reminding us that class decisions are not set in stone but subject to individual agency.

Research in the United States (Lareau, 2003), United Kingdom (Ball, 2003) and Australia (Doherty, 2009) have shown how middle-class parents use all means possible, investing both money and time to secure school advantage for their children, whether through enrolment in private schools or provision of cultural capital in the form of extracurricular activities. Providing print-rich homes and examples of reading are some ways through which parents pass on reading habits and diets (Neuman & Celano, 2012a). The boys' early exposure to books and reading resulted in their reading competence and willingness to explore various genres and reading material for their leisure reading. In the Singapore context, there seems to be little difference from the United States when it comes to university-educated parents making "concerted effort" to ensure the "transmission of differential advantages" (Lareau, 2003, p. 5) by encouraging their children to pick up reading, something that is well-suited to later success in school readings. Reading, as a form of cultural capital, may be more influential than the transmission of high culture in ensuring educational success (De Graaf, De Graaf, & Kraaykamp, 2000). Although both low-income and middle-class parents in Singapore invest much time and income in their children's education, the ability of middle-class parents with higher educational and economic resources to cultivate reading habits does provide their children with differential economic, social and cultural capital which contributes to the advantages in academic achievement (Teo, 2016).

The invisible network of resources, paradoxically, makes visible the resources that contribute to the making of a reader. It debunks the notion of a "natural" reader and highlights how access to resources and models of reading (in the form of parents and other family members, peers in school and outside of school), often available to middle-class children, may better prepare them to develop the reading identities so crucial to engaging in reading as lifelong practice. Being immersed in a habitus where reading is the norm predisposes a child towards reading, and children from lower socioeconomic backgrounds may be disadvantaged by their lack of access to meaningful ways of engaging with books and reading (Buckingham, Beaman, & Wheldall, 2014; Neuman & Celano, 2012a). Students from lower socioeconomic backgrounds who succeed in developing reading identities tend to come from homes that resemble middle-class homes (Harris & Graves, 2010; Lareau, 2003). Acknowledging these resources may help combat deficit constructions of students and allow teachers to develop specific strategies for helping all students learn. In the next section, I focus on how boys read, contrasting the reading practices of the weaker students from Tembusu Secondary with the reading practices of the strong readers from Ace Institution.

Boys reading books: complicating gendered reading practices

Social class needs to be understood at the intersection of other factors such as race, ethnicity and gender, all within the complexities of individual national boundaries. In this section, I bring gender into the equation, focusing specifically on how examining gender at the intersection of social class may provide insight into how and why boys read. In contrast to studies on girls' reading and identity practices (Cherland, 1994; Christian-Smith, 2001; Finders, 1997; Walkerdine, 1990), there have been fewer studies focused on the reading and identity practices of boys. Studies on boys' reading practices have tended to portray boys as uninterested in narratives and more interested in plot-driven stories if they read at all (e.g., Millard, 1997; Simpson, 1996). This simplistic view of boys' and girls' reading habits and practices neglects the complexity of boys' reading practices at the intersection of race and ethnicity and social class (Moss, 2007; Smith & Wilhelm, 2002; Solsken, 1993; Weaver-Hightower, 2003; Young & Bozo, 2003).

Gender can influence perception and propensity to read. In Cherland's (1994) ethnographic study of a group of sixth form girls' reading practices, she demonstrated how the girls' identification as readers and their relations with books were shaped by their social worlds. Within their Canadian suburban community, the girls learn to read as a gendered way of being "good" in comparison to the boys who were measured by their sporting excellence rather than their bookish preferences. However, in the previous section, I demonstrated how the high-achieving Ace Institution readers do not perceive reading as a feminine activity, in part due to their family backgrounds and reading histories. As such, gendered ways of reading must be understood in relation to class and other intersections of race and ethnicity. In this section, I focus on the reading practices of academically weaker boys from lower social classes from a social perspective to illuminate how class background and reading practices align to discourage the development of particular reading identities for some boys.

In Moss's (2007) study of gendered reading practices in four primary schools, she observes how attention to the social practices of reading at the intersection of gender and reading competence reveals nuanced differences within and across gender reading practices. Detailed observations of students' reading in school, together with interview data, reveal that boys and girls placed in different levels of reading proficiency exercised different choices over what to read and how to read. Working with the 7–9 age group, she identified three categories of readers: (1) readers who *can and do read* freely, (2) readers who *can but don't read* freely, and (3) readers who *can't yet and don't read* freely. Students who *can and do read* are students whom the researchers in the study observed choose to read voluntarily, whereas students who *can but don't read* are proficient readers but seldom chose to read on their own. Students who *can't yet and* don't are those with a lower reading proficiency who are not interested in reading. Examining the reading practices of boys and girls with lower reading proficiencies, she notes that their different responses to their classification as weak readers lead to uneven learning opportunities.

Using the examples of students engaging in free reading activities, Moss illustrates how the *can't yet* boys' preference for non-linear non-fiction was a deliberate choice to mask their low reading proficiency. The non-linear, informational texts allow for selective focus, and the visuals provide a form of scaffolding for conversation with other students, allowing the boys to maintain their social status as experts in the subject area even if they were not experts in reading. Their lack of practice in sustained reading during free reading did not allow them to improve their reading proficiency. This concern with social status is less of a concern for *can't yet* girls, who were less worried about their social standing. In fact, female students seem to enjoy turning the reading experience into play, choosing to practice proficiency reading in make-believe school situations. Drawing on Bente Elkjaer's (1992) work, Moss writes

> . . . where knowledge is at a premium, boys gain considerable authority from being able to claim to know most, and will prioritise saving face . . . By contrast, girls seem to find it easier to be on the receiving end of others' help, at less immediate cost to their self-esteem.
>
> (p. 145)

Because boys are less willing to admit what they do not know, it is more difficult to find out the learning gaps. On the other hand, whereas it is easier to find out what girls don't already know, there is a risk that others around them may underestimate their general knowledge or skill. This explains the different text choices of weak boys and girls, for whom different use of texts and conversation around texts serve as forms of interaction with friends.

In contrast to the weak boy readers, proficient boy readers who are able to sustain reading of lengthier linear texts may have different reasons for their choice of books. During free reading periods, they may choose easier chapter books to complete them within the allocated time for reading but possess the ability to complete longer and more difficult books. The proficient boy readers tended to be flexible readers who could browse through non-linear non-fiction to engage in conversation with their friends at school but who were also able to engage in sustained reading of linear fiction. The ability and choice to read chapter books also allowed these boys to make value judgements about their "superior" reading competency and dedication: "Proficiency and choice elide so that the chapter-book reader becomes at once more proficient, but also more dedicated to the act of reading. Readers who choose this kind of text have the stamina and the serious commitment to the activity which others lack" (Moss, 2007, p. 154). Her subsequent study of the library borrowing records of the students at one of the schools revealed that there was no significant difference in the titles that boys and girls loaned out over the course of a year. Boys who were avid readers borrowed fiction, and by contrast, it was those who read least at home who were most likely to spend time on non-fiction at school. Similarly, the Ace readers were able to flexibly and purposefully select texts for their own leisure reading; on the other hand, the weaker readers at Tembusu found it difficult to complete the books allocated for their Sustained Silent Reading (SSR) periods and, instead, shirked the task of reading by feigning engagement or remaining quiet during reading periods.

Moss's study illustrates how examining reading from social perspectives at the intersection of gender and reading proficiency can provide insight into differential reading choices and practices. Reading instruction must address issues specific to each group of students for success. Social class is relevant here as there is a high chance that students from poorer homes begin school already disadvantaged in their reading competence and are more likely to fall behind (Buckingham et al., 2014).

36 Becoming *a reader*

Students who are less competent in their reading are less likely to identify as readers (Hicks, 2002; Moss, 2007) and less likely to engage with activities that could encourage their development as readers.

Contrasting access to reading models and resources using the *invisible network of resources* between the avid readers at Ace and the weak readers at Tembusu, it was clear that the Tembusu boys' habitus did not include intensive immersion in books and reading (See Table 2.2).

The three Normal Academic boys interviewed (Nate, Max and Yi Han) were identified by their teachers as academically weak and self-identified through the survey as non-readers. When I requested via Whatsapp for photographs of their bookshelves at home, only Yi Han responded. Yi Han's visual documentation provided stark evidence of the different home resources for reading. Yi Han shared that he had four books, which he had been inspired to purchase during his primary school days when Geronimo Stilton and *The Diary of a Wimpy Kid* were the rage among his classmates. The other two boys, Max and Nate, informed me during our focus group that they had no books nor bookshelves at home. In contrast, although I did not obtain photographic records of books or bookshelves from the Ace boys, their conversations were littered with references to books and

Table 2.2 Tembusu boys' reading resources

No.	Reading Resources		Examples
1	Family	1	Max: I don't think anybody reads.
		2	Nate: They read the newspapers.
2	Recommendations	1	Nate: I don't really recommend books or get book recommendations from my friends.
		2	Yi Han: I bought Geronimo Stilton because my friends were reading them.
3	School	1	Nate: For school books (novels from the school's reading programme), I never finished them. . ... To do the reflection, I just read the beginning, middle and end.
		2	Max: The only book I finished was *Charlie and the Chocolate Factory*. It was interesting, and funny.
4	Bookstores	1	Yi Han: I go to Popular bookstore. To buy textbooks and stationery.
		2	Nate: I don't really go to the bookstore.
5	Libraries	1	Max: I went to the public library with my friends during the school holidays. We walked around a bit and then went home.
		2	Yi Han: I don't go to the school library. During recess, I rather go to the games room (beside the school canteen).
6	Other media	1	I watched *Ah Boys to Men* (a made- and set-in-Singapore movie about a group of boys growing up during their compulsory National Service stint as soldiers).
		2	Yi Han: I watched *The Lion, the Witch and the Wardrobe* on Channel 5 (a free-to-air channel on Singapore TV) so I think the book might be quite good.

bookshelves at home. For example, Michael shared that he "shared a bookshelf with [my] two older brothers and read all their books", and Robert talked about his grandfather's "Gerald Durrell collection" that he used to read when he visited his grandparents. Table 2.1, provided earlier, also illustrates the wealth of print the Ace boys had access to.

In the following focus group discussion, Max and Nate explain why they did not send me any photographs of their bookshelves.

Chin: Only Yi Han sent me the photographs of his bookshelves. Why didn't you guys send yours?
Max: I don't have any books at home.
Nate: I don't have . . .
Chin: None at all?
Max: Really. No books.
Nate: I don't buy books. I don't read.
Chin: Then what do you do in your free time?
Nate: Play computer games.
Chin: Hmmm . . . OK, so Yi Han, tell me about your books. Why did you buy these books?
YH: I don't know. It looked interesting. My friends were reading Geronimo Stilton in primary school, so I decided to get one for myself.

(Group Interview, 22 May 2014)

From the discussion, it is clear that books and reading are not a priority for Max and Nate. For the more earnest Yi Han, he shared that he spent his savings on three books from the Geronimo Stilton series and one from the *Diary of a Wimpy Kid* series because he was motivated by friends who were reading books in the same series. They explained that reading and books was not a priority for them, and as Table 2.2 illustrates, they had little opportunity to engage in social activities around books and were less motivated to think about books and reading as leisure or a pleasurable activity. Using the network of resources as a beginning point for measuring the amount of resources available to each boy, it was clear that these boys had qualitatively fewer resources to encourage the construction of a reading identity from an early age. Yi Han, who does not identify as a reader in the school-wide survey, reads when he is motivated to, usually by his friends. Moreover, whereas he does not see his parents reading, he does see his older siblings reading some young adult novels and his grandparents reading the Chinese newspapers. In comparison, Max and Nate, who also identified as non-readers, have fewer reading examples. To the survey question, "If you see your sisters or brothers read, what do they read?" Nate reports in a matter-of-fact tone: "They don't read. But study only" (reflecting a typical Singapore tendency to create a dichotomy between reading and studying). This lack of excitement about books is visible in the interviews where the boys found it difficult to recall memorable experiences of reading and books; in contrast, most of the interviews with the Ace Institution boys were populated with memories of books and sharing about recent books read. This qualitative difference in home backgrounds partially explains the Tembusu boys' resistance to reading as a valid and interesting leisure activity.

Yet, not all weak readers were non-readers or could not be persuaded to read. Yi Han shared that he had attempted to visit the public library at least once during the school holidays to borrow books. Although he described himself as a non-reader who did not like to read, he stated in his survey that he would "be engrossed" if [he] found a book he liked. When asked what books he liked, he communicated that

> I like reading those young reader storybooks like Geronimo Stilton and *Diary of the Wimpy Kid* which was during primary school :p I read very less books as I was choosy on which one to read and which one is interesting to me. To me, if it is interesting, I will read it. I will read it at a slower rate :p
> (*Whatsapp* communication, April 26, 2014)

This attitude was echoed in the descriptive portion of the survey data, where students were asked to describe themselves as readers: students who did not identify as readers or declared that they did not like reading often described themselves as being willing to read if they found books that appealed to them. What follows are three quotes from the survey data that illustrate the point.

> "I like to read things that interest me."
> (Noah, 14 years old)

> "If I like the book, I'd read at least 10 pages once I started. But if I dislike it as it is boring, I can't even hold my eyes on it for more than two pages."
> (Shann, 14 years old)

> "I do not see myself as a reader. I only like books from Russell Lee [who writes horror stories and is often considered a non-literary read by teachers and students themselves]."
> (James, 14 years old)

For Yi Han, Max and Nate, it was clear that interest was a driving factor that motivated their reading. When probed about whether they completed the allocated books for the school's reading programme, both Nate and Max confessed that the only book they had completed reading when they were in Secondary One was Roald Dahl's *Charlie and the Chocolate Factory* (out of about 10 allocated titles over the course of one year). Yi Han shared that he attempted to read most of the books but that *Charlie and the Chocolate* Factory was one of the few he managed to complete. Nate shared that the book was "so funny" that he "brought it home and finished it". The school's reading programme provided two 20-minute periods for SSR, and each student had six weeks to complete the reading of the allocated book, yet the boys were not able to complete most of the books (titles included *Charlie and the Chocolate Factory* by Roald Dahl, *Totto Chan* by Tetsuko Kuroyanagi, *Chinese Cinderella* by Adeline Yen Mah, *The Lion, the Witch and the Wardrobe* by C. S. Lewis and *Marley and Me* by John Grogan). The school's reading programme was commendable in attempting to provide a wide range of books for all students. However, given the low reading proficiency of the boys, they would need more time than that allocated during class to complete the books. In addition, they needed to be sufficiently interested in the book to bring it home and complete the reading, which was what they did with *Charlie and the Chocolate Factory*.

Their description of their reading of *Charlie and the Chocolate Factory*, where they brought the books home and completed them over a short period of sustained reading, was driven by the pleasure that the books gave to them and resembles the behaviour of engaged readers (Wilhelm, 2016). In Wilhelm's study of engaged readers, he described different kinds of pleasure brought by reading and suggests that "immersive play pleasure", the "pleasure you get from living through a story and getting totally lost in a book", is a pre-requisite pleasure to encourage reading. He notes that schools tended to over-emphasise "intellectual pleasure", which is the pleasure of being able to figure things out. For the Tembusu boys, it was the immersive play pleasure of reading *Charlie and the Chocolate Factory* that encouraged them to sustain the reading of the book. If the emphasis is on encouraging students to sustain reading through immersive play experiences, reading more Roald Dahl and other forms of "easy" reading such as series books can help to cultivate interest while encouraging sustained reading.

Despite the good intentions of the English department, the reading programme failed to take into account the need for motivation to encourage weak boy readers to sustain reading. Although the SSR programme encouraged avid and competent readers to increase their reading and the variety of books read, weaker boy readers did not benefit as much from the task. They would flip through the book and expertly use the information provided in the blurb and last pages to complete the required reflection. Reading for pleasure is perhaps too often neglected in the secondary classroom as there is perhaps an assumption that adolescent students will read on their own or will no longer require encouragement to read. Keeping in mind that it is engaged reading that is linked to improved reading competence and academic achievement (Kirsch et al., 2002; OECD, 2010a), there needs to be more dedicated attention to how to encourage engaged reading. The implementation of a reading programme, when examined carefully, may not actually benefit the target students.

In their research on the expectations of post-primary pupils and teachers, Laurenson, McDermott, Sadleir, and Meade (2015) found that whereas post-primary students still expected to have instituted reading periods as they had in primary schools, their teachers' perceptions of reading were not so much free or independent reading as reading instruction, where students would engage in close reading of short texts in teacher-led sessions. Within the Tembusu context, the emphasis was on English as a functional skill, and reading was linked to such instrumental rather than pleasurable purposes. In their answers to an open-ended, school-wide survey on reading practices (Q5. Please explain why reading is important to you), students tended toward a functional (78.5%) rather than aesthetic view of reading (see Table 2.3 for coding details). Functional views towards reading suggest a pragmatic, instrumentalist view, whereas an aesthetic view implies reading for pleasure (Rosenblatt, 1995). This mirrors the school's official discourse on the importance of reading for the purposes of academic achievement. Clearly, the students had absorbed official discourses of the importance of reading, although they may not be sufficiently persuaded of its value to their own lives or even to their grades. When probed about whether they saw reading as contributing to academic achievement (Q6: Does reading help you do better in school?), only 44.3% were certain it influenced their grades positively; 52.1% were uncertain; and 3.7% were sure reading did not help them do better in school. Because such a large percentage was unconvinced of the actual usefulness of reading to academic grades, an argument that reading would help them improve academically is unlikely to persuade them to fully invest in the activity of reading (see Loh, 2015a, for further details on the survey findings).

For the Tembusu boys who did not have the home resources for building reading identities, school support for building a reading identity is very important. Successful reading programmes often leverage on intrinsic motivation and choice (Francois, 2013; Ivey & Broaddus, 2001; Lee, 2011) to cultivate both student desire to read and competency at reading (Cremin, Mottram, Collins, Powerll, & Safford, 2014). However, Tembusu's more functional approach of allocating texts to students failed to engage the low-proficiency boys. Requiring students to account for their readings through mandatory reflections only added to the perception that this was a school task and not something to be done for enjoyment. In contrast to the Ace Institution boys', whose regular access to books at home mediated their skill and will to attempt school readings, the Tembusu boys required more encouragement to read. Although providing access to books in school is an important element of supporting students' reading habits and practices, it is more essential to help students by providing them with suitably engaging books and teaching them the skills to select books they would enjoy. The Ace Institution students' access to a wide range of books from an early age prepared them to select books that they would be interested in and cultivated a disposition

Table 2.3 Sample responses for functional and aesthetic views towards reading

Functional View	Aesthetic View
It improves my vocabulary and grammar.	Reading is important to me because I use my extra time to read books and relax.
Reading expands our knowledge as well as improves our grammar.	It brings me to another world of fantasy, things that will not happen in reality.
It gives us a better command of the language and also helps us to converse better with each other.	It triggers the imagination, and reading is interesting.

of willingness to explore new genres. For the Tembusu boys who come from homes where there have not been intensive immersion in books and mentorship in reading, there is a need to "unlevel the playing field" (Neuman & Celano, 2012b, p. 18). In their study of two public libraries in Philadelphia in the United States, Neuman and Celano point out that "equal community-based resources do not create equal opportunity" (p. 18) because poor students come from homes where class- and culture-based parenting practices may disadvantage their learning. In the same manner, the presence of a reading programme or a school library does not necessarily mean that all students are utilising the resources in the same manner. For students from home backgrounds where reading is not the norm, more needs to be invested to help them develop reading identities.

Developing a reading identity

This chapter makes visible the process of *becoming* a reader, focusing on the reading practices of the Ace and Tembusu boys. The invisible network of resources (consisting of home, peer, library, bookstore, school and other media) makes explicit the various nodes where intensive immersion in books and reading, particularly at an early age, encourages the development of a reading identity. The middle-class Ace boys, growing up in reading homes, learnt to see reading as a valid leisure activity. Through personal engagement with intensive reading, they come to see themselves as readers.

In contrast to the rich print experiences of the Ace boys, the low-achieving Tembusu boys from low-income homes have less access to books at home and fewer opportunities to see adults engaged in meaningful reading. This pattern reflects findings from a recent national survey on reading conducted: Adults with only primary school or no education were the least likely to have read a book in the past 12 months (National Arts Council, 2015). Students with such parents are thus less likely to have access to reading examples, in part through working parents' lack of time and knowledge to get them started.

To understand that a reading identity is developed through immersion in a habitus which values such activities helps educators to understand better why certain students may lack the will (in addition to the skills) to read. Certainly, early childhood education and primary education would be the best places to provide the resources to cultivate a reading identity at school. However, one cannot assume that all students learn to read well by the time they are 13; rather, there needs to be a continual emphasis on the pleasures of reading to entice adolescent students busy with other commitments and media to want to read and grow both in reading and life competency as a result of their reading. Instead of focusing solely on reading instruction, schools need to concentrate on concurrently building a reading culture where students see reading as pleasurable and meaningful (Cremin et al., 2014; Krashen, 2004; Laurenson et al., 2015). Unfortunately, reading programmes designed from functional perspectives tend to include accountability features such as tests, reflections, and assignments that send a contradictory message. Yet, in reality, an engaged reader reads not to complete an assignment but because the task at home is enjoyable and purposeful. Strategies for encouraging reading need to take into account the student profile and identification as a reader to help shape students' understanding of themselves as engaged readers, despite their reading competency.

To help students build reader identities, to construct a school habitus where students can begin to see themselves as readers, teachers need to become more competent readers themselves (Cremin et al., 2014), able to help students with book selection and modelling what it means to be a reader. Knowledge of books and adolescent reading habits, together with a specific background and observational knowledge of one's students, will allow for customisation of reading programmes for different students. For example, for the Normal Academic boys from Tembusu, reading more Roald Dahl would have been a way to affirm their reading competency and engage them in further reading. The strategy of flooding students with a wide range of books from different genres worked for the more competent readers but not for the lower-proficiency readers who had less linguistic and cultural capital to plug into texts. Reading around authors and series books can encourage students' sustained interest and help them build stamina in reading. For the lower-proficiency boys, it was not flexibility but familiarity that series books or authors provide that can help them build confidence, leading to greater interest and competence in reading. Series books (Jones, 2015), magazines (Gabriel, Allington, & Billen, 2012) and comics (Worthy, Moorman, & Turner, 1999) are all valid for encouraging reading, and students can be encouraged to engaged with other longer texts or different texts as they build up their reading stamina and competence.

Wilhelm (2016) points to the tendency of schools to prioritise the intellectual pleasure that books afford but notes that "the first and pre-requisite kind of pleasure" that readers experience is typically the "immersive pleasure of play" (p. 34). This immersive pleasure of play is the feeling of "living through a story and getting totally lost in a book" and can serve as a bridge to other kinds of pleasures. Popular culture books and young adult novels (Ivey & Johnston, 2013), although sometimes scorned in the English classroom, can help lead students into the immersive world of reading. Such books can serve as a bridge into reading and motivate students to read more difficult and varied texts as they familiarise themselves with sustained reading and build reading stamina. Reading is a "socially framed" activity where collective institutional and community processes "shape reading practices by authoritatively defining what is worth reading and how to read it" (Long, 1993, p. 192), and schools need to create an environment where students can see themselves as readers. Whether students see their reading as valid and whether they see themselves as readers are very much tied to social conceptions of what counts as "good reading." Oprah's book club is an example of how non-readers can be enticed to engage in reading as a valid leisure activity and demonstrates how expanding definitions of what makes a reader and what counts as valid reading can engage wider audiences in reading, and adolescent readers need to be persuaded that reading is an activity worth engaging in. By including a wide variety of genres to expand school definitions of what counts as good reading, schools can begin to validate adolescent identifications as readers and from there encourage students to read more and to read more widely.

In the Singapore context, the dominant discourse driving reading practices and programmes often focuses on the functional-pragmatic value of reading, and much classroom time is allocated to reading instruction, mostly in the form of teaching students to excel in reading comprehension. This examination-oriented emphasis may spill over to extensive reading programmes in schools, often adapted to include an accountability element in the form of reflections or summaries as evidence of reading. This need for accountability goes against the grain of extensive reading principles and emphasises to students the functional, outcome-driven aspect of reading rather than pleasurable, institutional learning for lifelong learning (Wolf & Bokhorst-Heng, 2008).

Whether students read or not often depends on the social life of reading in their homes, classrooms and communities. The Ace Institution boys, who identified themselves as engaged readers, were surrounded by people who read, who read to them, or who read with them from a young age. Understanding that reading is a social activity can help educators reframe the design of reading programmes to prioritise creating spaces for social activity around books. Students should have opportunities to select books of their choice, to discuss books read and to recommend them to friends without the need for accountability in the form of tests, reflections or book reports. Allowing students to choose their own books can help with motivation and sustaining reading. However, it is important that a wide variety of books are available and teachers know enough about a wide variety of books and their students to make recommendations (Cremin et al., 2014). Focusing on facilitating student conversations around books can encourage students to attend to other people's perspectives and to understand the world better through their engagement with literature (Ivey, 2014).

For reading programmes to be truly successful, schools need to find means other than grades for evaluation. In her work on reading, Calkins (2001) suggests that in schools and classrooms with strong reading cultures, children and adolescents should "author rich literate selves" and "want the life of a reader and envision that life for themselves" (pp. 8–9). Schools can measure their schools' reading culture by observing whether reading permeates the classroom and out-of-class programmes, measuring students' motivation to read and observing if there is constant social activity around books and reading (evidenced in part by peer sharing about books and classroom conversations about books) (Francois, 2015). Non-negotiable and sustained curriculum time needs to be put aside for students to engage in the 'readerly' activities already mentioned. Even though early childhood and the primary years are crucial to providing opportunities to level students' learning to read and loving to read through exposure to rich literature, encouraging these habits of reading continues to be important in early adolescence.

Focusing on the everyday reading practices of students at home and school reveals that students are socialised into becoming readers and learn ways of responding to books from a young age. This perspective highlights that not all students begin and continue schooling with equal resources for constructing a reading identity that is crucial to reading engagement and academic success. Rather than blaming students for not wanting to read, it might be more fruitful to examine how to create spaces and programmes to cultivate reading identities, an idea that will be discussed in Chapter 4. The invisible network of resources identifies areas where teachers and schools can design targeted approaches to improve reading. For example, schools can entice students to read by drawing them in with book-related movies or video games such as *The Hunger Games* or *The Life of Pi*. Furthermore, schools can work with families or think about programmes to encourage peer reading and sharing. By acknowledging that students come to school differently resourced and, as such, respond to books and reading programmes differently, schools will be able to design more nuanced and targeted approaches to encourage reading.

Note

1 Singapore colloquial term for "very enjoyable".

3 Singaporean boys constructing global literate selves
School-nation connections

Drawing on the data from the Ace Institution study, this chapter explores how the elite boys from Ace Institution construct global literate selves for a global market. Increasingly, in this "new work order" (Gee, Hull, & Lankshear, 1996), it is the "symbolic-analysts" (Reich, 1991) or "creative class" (Florida, 2002) or "knowledge workers" (Druckner, 1969) with the ability to harness knowledge for innovation who are valued within nations and globally for their ability to contribute to economically lucrative industries. Individuals who are special, specialised, anchored or adaptable, and thereby marketable, are preferred in this "flattened world" (Friedman, 2005). This logic has led to national educational investments targeted to reap economic benefits, with intense investments in creating highly-skilled, globally-mobile and networked individuals. Brown, Lauder and Ashton (2011) argue that the "global auction" for jobs has led to increasing competition across borders, and education may not be fulfilling its role of ensuring the link between educational investment and economic rewards in developed countries, despite the public discourse that individuals who upgrade their skills will be able to improve themselves to meet the requirements of the global knowledge-based economy.

This argument, driven by the neoliberal logic of increased competition in a meritocratic society demanding ever-higher skills development and credentialing (R. Collins, 1979), hides the fact that access to such skills needs much investment and effort that some individuals may be able to afford more than others. Bauman (1998) points to this stratification of access and opportunity where one's starting point determines the ability to move up the social (global) ladder.

> All of us are, willy-nilly, by design or default, on the move. We are on the move even if physically, we stay put: immobility is not a realistic option in a world of permanent change. And yet the effects of that new condition are radically unequal. Some of us become fully and truly 'global'; some are fixed in their 'locality' – a predicament neither pleasurable nor endurable in which the 'globals' set the tone and compose the rules of the life game.
>
> (p. 2)

Thus, wealthy transnational individuals pursue overseas education or passports (Ong, 1999; Waters, 2006) to manage their risks in an uncertain world (Beck, 1992), whereas others may be less outwardly or upwardly mobile as a result of their life chances.

Ultimately, individuals who benefit the most in this neoliberal economy of globalised flows are those who are able to easily straddle different worlds. Drawing on Robert Merton's work, Hannerz (1990) uses the term "cosmopolitans" to distinguish these global travellers from the "locals" who are rooted in place. Hannerz describes cosmopolitans as people who are able to move at ease between different cultural contexts, having acquired an orientation towards engaging with the other. They possess a greater understanding of diversity and of the need for the coexistence of various cultures within the individual person. For Hannerz, these cosmopolitans are "'the new class' people with credentials, decontextualised cultural capital" (p. 246). Unlike those who are tied to a specific place and whose influence rests on *whom* they know rather than *what* they know, cosmopolitans possess knowledge less tied to others and are able to recontextualise their work in different cultural contexts (see Appiah, 2006, for discussion of the reformuation of the term "cosmopolitanism" in global contexts; B. Cheah & Robbins, 1998; Lam, 2006a).

Cosmopolitan as a concept has been revived in recent discussions as a way of thinking beyond the nation (e.g., Appiah, 2006; Cheah & Robbins, 1998). Tomlinson (1999) suggests that cosmopolitanism is a disposition where individuals are not limited by concerns of one's immediate locality but are able to recognise "global belonging, involvement and responsibility and can integrate these broader concerns into everyday life practices" (p. 184). For Tomlinson, cosmopolitans need to be "simultaneously universalists and pluralists" (p. 194) in their view of and in their relation to both nation and world. As such, the term "cosmopolitan" can be said to apply not just to people who are based outside their country of origin but even to those who live and work in cosmopolitan cities such as New York, London, Hong Kong and Singapore, where an eye towards the world has become part of the everyday practice of living and working.

Learning to become *cosmopolitan* is part of elite schooling, and this chapter examines how the Ace Institution boys cultivate dispositions of cosmopolitanism through their reading and other literacy practices. Their construction of selves as global-literate citizens is very much aligned with articulated national policy to cultivate cosmopolitan elites able to plug into global markets and through that contribute to the national economy. The rhetoric of meritocracy requires that every child be afforded the opportunity to acquire the kinds of reading and literacy skills required for global markets; in practice, national and institutional practices align with middle-class practices and investments to allow students attending elite schools a better chance of acquiring the sort of fluent and flexible literacies prized in global markets. Whereas not all elite school students come from middle-class homes, there is a greater proportion of students with at least one university-educated parent in top schools in Singapore, compared to neighbourhood schools (Ramesh, 2011). Mirroring worldwide trends, middle-class parents may see sending their children to elite schools as a form of risk management for an uncertain future (Doherty, 2009; Reay, Crozier, & James, 2013; Vidovich & Yap, 2008; Waters, 2006; Windle & Stratton, 2012). The ability of middle-class parents with greater economic, social and cultural capital to invest in their children's futures disadvantages lower-income students without the same resources.

Within the Singapore schooling system, this selective cosmopolitanism is not an accident; rather, the training of a selected minority to develop skills and dispositions relevant for a global world is part of the government's "tactical globalization" (Koh, 2010) to ensure Singapore remains competitive and relevant in a constantly shifting world. Ye and Nylander (2015), from a data set of the institutional origins of 580 Singaporean government scholars, trace the "sponsored mobility" of elite school students whose schools prime them for scholarship paths by providing the "informational capital" required for access to Oxbridge and eventually to the higher strata of the Singapore Public Service. There is "concerted effort" not just at family but also at national and institutional levels to provide cultural capital for the best and the brightest in the land to excel.

In Chapter 2, I explained how the invisible network of resources forms the habitus that supports middle-class children's construction of reading identities. In this chapter, I show how what is being shaped is not just a reading identity but a particular kind of reading identity that prepares some students better than others for projecting themselves as global-literate citizens. The types of books read, as well as ways of reading and communicating about books, serve as forms of cultural capital. Through texts read, students learn to see themselves as particular kinds of readers, and project themselves as particular kinds of persons (J. Collins & Blot, 2003). Reading the right kind of book provides the right kind of cultural capital for fitting in with the crowd. For Bourdieu, the possession of a critical attitude and the ability to distinguish between high and low art and to decide one's superior preference as a matter of taste is in fact "social necessity made second nature" (Bourdieu, 1984, p. 474) are ways the middle classes may mark their superiority. In Janice Radway's (1997) examination of the popularity of the Book-of-the-Month Club, a subscription-based book delivery service founded in 1926, she pointed to how the readers saw their reading of these selected books as an entry point into literary discretion and as providing a point of identification as middle class. These attitudes towards books, or "long lasting dispositions of the mind and body" (Bourdieu, 1986, p. 47), are forms of embodied cultural capital that are convertible into economic capital in certain conditions. In the schooling context, familiarity with certain kinds of texts can translate to educational advantage which results in the acquisition of institutionalised cultural capital – educational qualifications.

Competence in traditional literacies remains important (Warshauer, 2007), but more important is a way of reading, writing and thinking that projects the individual as a worldly global citizen. The ability to communicate with multicultural others through the demonstration of one's knowledge of the world (partly acquired through texts) is another typically unacknowledged aspect of language learning. These unacknowledged dispositions of worldliness, creativity, criticality and flexibility (together with their mastery of basic skills) are inscribed on the Ace students through their home and school practices and are a form of embodied cultural capital that allow the students to position themselves as globally literate individuals, ready to plug into international markets, and, in that way, contribute eventually to individual and national economic well-being.

Although more individuals are acquiring basic literacy skills, ever-higher standards of learning push up the expectations for what counts as basic literacy (Gee, Hull, & Lankshear, 1996). Increasing access to education has only inflated the credential market (Brown et al., 2011; R. Collins, 1979), leading anxious parents to intensify the search for better educational portfolios, better schools, and better degrees to ensure their children's success in the "risk society" (Beck, 1992), beginning in early childhood with the search for the "right" childcare and enrichment activities. This parental anxiety is shared by the nation: If individuals are human capital meant to contribute to the economic well-being of the country, there needs to be a tight alignment between projected manpower requirements and training. Educational investment is thus perceived as providing capital in the long run for both the nation and individual.

The popularity of elite schooling results from the perception that students need to compete at international levels to maintain or improve their status in a highly competitive world. The increased wave of research on elite schooling in various contexts, including the United States (Demerath, 2009; Howard, 2010a; Khan, 2012), France (Draelants & Darchy-Koechlin, 2011) and former British colonies such as Australia, South Africa, Singapore and India (e.g., Epstein, 2014; Fahey, 2014; Kenway & Koh, 2013; Meadmore & Meadmore, 2004), springs in part from the notion that "studying up" is one way to better understand and generate critical insight into how advantage (and disadvantage) is reproduced (Howard, 2010b), an increasingly pressing issue in a stratified world. Koh and Kenway (2012) have pointed out in their study of an elite all-boys' school in Singapore how the school's educational logic is directed by the national habitus, which requires the boys to see Singapore's success as necessarily tied to being global. As such, the construction of a cosmopolitan self is necessary for these students primed for leadership and global markets. At the level of practice, the students are socialised into leadership and a sense of *noblesse oblige* through the school's curriculum, service learning and leadership programmes. Institutional habitus thus prepares the elite students to serve in the national interest.

In this chapter, I zoom in to the Ace Institution's schoolboys' reading practices to highlight how specific powerful reading practices are reproduced through schooling. For the elite schoolboys in this chapter, national, institutional and personal habitus cohere to help them construct global literate identities suitable for cosmopolitan projections in a global world.

Cultivating the cosmopolitan Singaporean

The terms "cosmopolitans" and "heartlanders" were coined by former prime minister Goh Chok Tong (1999) to describe two kinds of Singaporeans during the National Day Rally in his speech titled "First World Economy, World-Class Home." Although the distinction is no longer fashionable in the official and public domain, it may well capture the mind-set that lingers in Singapore's differentiated educational policy and practices (see L.-C. Ho, 2012; Lim, 2014). This uncomplicated division of Singaporeans into two types with specific traits and dispositions (one local and the other global) generated much controversy when first used: Cosmopolitans have an "international outlook that enable them to work and be comfortable anywhere in the world", whereas the heartlanders are the "conservative majority" who tend to be more rooted to the nation and concerned with their daily bread and butter than political issues. Cosmopolitans are perceived as more likely to treat Singapore as a "hotel" rather than a "home" because of their global marketability, whereas heartlanders tend to see Singapore as home because of their attachment to home or their lack of choice (E. Ho, 2006). At the same time, because cosmopolitans are able to generate wealth through their skills and connections, they must be persuaded to regard Singapore as home and the world as their marketplace. Thus, whereas elite students are expected to become globetrotting cosmopolitans with international outlooks and skills to extend their economic reach beyond Singapore, heartlanders are less mobile and invariably tied to the nation by their absence of options.

English as a global linga franca (Graddol, 2006) is essential for plugging into international markets and for ensuring Singapore's success in the global marketplace. As such, the English language has long occupied a privileged position as the official language of education and business in Singapore (Gopinathan, 2003; Silver, 2005), and English fluency is a form of cultural capital. The importance of English is continually emphasised in public discourse, for example, through the Speak Good English Movement, a government campaign launched in 2000 to encourage "Singaporeans to speak grammatically correct English that is universally understood" (Speak Good English Movement, n.d.), and the founding of the English Language Institute of Singapore (ELIS) in 2011 to provide professional development to English teachers. The reason for language proficiency was underscored by founding prime minister Lee Kwan Yew in his opening address at the launch of ELIS in September 2011, where he reminded the audience that "English-speaking Singaporeans are sought after by MNCs, international organisations and NGOS because we can connect with the English-speaking environments", adding that

> [m]any countries in the region realize the importance of schooling their young in English . . . English schools are mushrooming in China, Thailand and Vietnam. . . .. Even native English speaking countries are concerned about the standard among their people. The UK and the US want to raise their standards of English.
>
> (K. Y. Lee, 2011)

More than just being able to converse in English, it is the ability to communicate in fluent and near native English proficiency that acts as a marker of cosmopolitanism. This desire to cultivate cosmopolitan English for a selected few is translated to a differentiated outcome in the Ministry of Education's (MOE's) official English curriculum. Whereas most students should learn to "[s]peak, write and represent in internationally acceptable English (Standard English) that is grammatical, fluent, mutually intelligible and appropriate for different purposes, audiences, contexts and cultures" (Ministry of Education, 2010, p. 10), "at least 20% will obtain a high degree of proficiency in English" to help "Singapore keep its edge in a range of profession." From this 20%, there should be a smaller group who will "achieve mastery in their command of the language that is no different from the best in English-speaking countries" (p. 6). Possession of English fluency as such is one mark of the cosmopolitan Singaporean, cultural capital with value for global markets.

The view of English language teaching in Singapore has tended to be skills oriented. Historically, the reason for this divide is the official perception of English language as the language of commerce and the mother tongue languages of Chinese, Malay and Tamil as the languages for the transmission of Asian cultural values (Gopinathan, 1980, 2003; Silver, 2005; Velayutham, 2007). This dichotomy between skills and values has led to the unusual division between the teaching of English language and English literature at the secondary school, with English language privileged as the primary language of education and business, and English literature (henceforth, referred to as "Literature") relegated to the aesthetic study of texts (Choo, 2013). Although Literature was a compulsory part of curriculum time, it was made an optional O-level subject in the early 1990s (Loh, 2013a; J. Tan & Gopinathan, 2000). Fewer students choose to offer Literature, partly because of the perception that it is a difficult subject to score in and thus should be left to elite school students already proficient in the English language (Poon, 2007). This view was enforced in a speech by then Education Minister Lee Yock Suan in 1995, where he suggested that "*brighter* students should study literature" (Unknown Author, 1995, headline from newspaper article, emphasis mine). Although official perspectives may have shifted since then, the fear that students with lower English proficiency would not do well in the subject remains the sentiments of some teachers, students and parents (Ng, 2013). As such, the study of literature typically tends to be associated with elite students or students who are already fluent in the language.

Curriculum distinctions: the IBDP curriculum and the Ace literate identity

Curriculum can be a form of cultural capital, although what counts as curriculum of the elite may differ according to contexts, often determined by the kinds of examinations that students eventually have to take to qualify for higher education (Cookson & Persell, 1985). Curriculum documents and textbooks legitimise ideologies, identities and beliefs (Apple, 1990, 1992; Christian-Smith, 2001; Luke, 1988), and the projection of a preferred national self is conveyed through the choice of national curricular and textual resources such as basal readers, school textbooks and canonical literary texts (J. Collins & Blot, 2003; Corse, 1997;

Luke, 1988). Kliebard (2004) has shown, through a historical examination of changes in the American curriculum, how interest groups struggle to shape what counts as relevant knowledge for each generation of students. These chosen texts are not neutral but represent a "selective tradition" (Williams, 1977), an ideological perspective about what matters to the dominant group in each community, a contested social imagery (Rizvi, 2008) of nation and world. The national curriculum shapes not just what counts but who counts, with policies determining who has access to various ways of learning. In addition to the kinds of texts read, how these texts are read also forms part of the curriculum distinction for particular groups of students (Apple, 1990, 1992; J. Collins & Blot, 2003). Particular "ways with words" (Heath, 1986) may hold more currency for academic purposes.

In the highly centralised education of Singapore, where policy is closely aligned to manpower and economic goals, official curriculum is tightly scripted and constantly revised (OECD, 2010b; Teh, 2014), even if differently implemented at various schools. At the same time, national high-stakes assessment often drives the kinds of learning prioritised by teachers (Y. M. Cheah, 2002; Kramer-Dahl, 2007; Loh & Liew, 2016; Silver, Curdt-Christiansen, Wright, & Stinson, 2013). In comparison, Ace Institution as an IP school has the flexibility of crafting its own curriculum (Kang, 2008). The adoption of the IBDP, with its focus on global-mindedness, signalled the school's readiness for the world and future. Ace Institution distinguishes itself as a leader in the development of students' communicative and cultural capital by including Literature as a central component of the curriculum. All students on the IBDP route have to offer English A1, which is essentially literary study, and the importance of Literature at the IBDP level filters down to the Years One to Four curricula. This emphasis on communicative skills and cultural knowledge can be seen as part of the institutional habitus of the school. Habitus is a form of "socialized subjectivity" (Bourdieu & Wacquant, 1992, p. 126), where students come to see collective, or social, norms and goals as their own, and the institutional habitus creates a space for group privileging of particular norms and goals. The institutional habitus (Reay, David, & Ball, 2001), "understood as the impact of a cultural group or social class on an individual's behaviour as it is mediated through an organization" (McDonough, 1996 in Reay, David, & Ball, 2001), consists of the ethos, values and expectations of the school. Institutional habitus plays an important role insofar as it structures individuals' perceptions and expectations of choice and contributes to students' understanding of the purpose of education (for them) and their role in the wider world. Ace Institution's institutional habitus, comprising discourses of excellence and distinction, tradition and progressiveness and rooted in cosmopolitanism and distinctive linguistic skills, is reflected in the boys' competencies, demeanour and attitudes. The institutional habitus of cultivating well-read, fluent and confident English speakers is in line with the national habitus of cultivating cosmopolitan citizens able to cross economic and cultural borders.

Within this context of schooling, Ace boys are cultivating a particular kind of reading identity, shaped and approved by public policy and discourse, and by the institutional habitus, through the curriculum. The curriculum forms part of the institutional habitus of elite schools, attesting to students' knowledge and ways of thinking that would be relevant to students' excellent performance at higher levels of education. Student subjectivities are shaped by school text choices and preferred ways of reading (Apple, 1992), and the focus on literature (as a subject for elite students), more specifically world literature (as a subject for *cosmopolitan world citizens*) is a form of distinction for Ace students. Additionally, the broader assessment focus, with equal emphasis on oral, written and research skills, differs from the more traditional written assessments at the O-levels and A-level Cambridge examinations, two high-stakes examinations typically taken at 16 and 18 years old, respectively, and contributes to the construction of well-read and confident communicators.

The world focus of the IBDP curriculum, with its wide reading list, distinguishes the Ace student from other students. The dean of the English Department explained the rationale for their choice of the IBDP curriculum:

> . . . [B]ecause of the international nature of the IB, we have the World Literature component, which is very important. . . . Also, the whole curriculum is supposed to instil in students this ability to empathise with people, especially people's perspectives that are different from their own, to develop empathy, to develop tolerance and respect for other people's views. You also learn about other people's culture.

Here, the dean of the English Department highlights the deliberate choice of the IBDP curriculum because of its focus on world literature. Through their readings, Ace students construct an "imagined community" (B. Anderson, 1991) of the world that prepares them to participate as global citizens in a multicultural and diverse world. The study of world literature (which includes translated texts) is "to expose language A1 candidates to works from cultures and literary traditions of their own" and aims to "broaden candidates' perspectives through the study of works from other cultures and languages" (IBO, 2002, p. 2). In total, students will read at least five world literature texts out of a total of about 12 over two years.

This respect for other cultures, evidenced partly through the students' wide reading of world literature, prepares students to be "cultural omnivores" (Peterson & Kern, 1996) in their knowledge of key texts and ways of reading. Tracing the changing habits of consumption, Peterson and Kern note that rather than being mere consumers of highbrow culture, contemporary elites are more likely to demonstrate a discriminating omnivorousness towards consumption, a disposition better suited to an increasingly global world where globetrotters "make their way, in part by showing respect for the cultural expressions of others" (p. 906). Rather than marking elite status by what is consumed, elites distinguish themselves by the way they appreciate and critique culture.

The school curriculum cultivates the discerning elite in part through the choice of texts – to expose students to a wide range of texts from different parts of the world – and in part through the assessment practices that focus on both oral and written competence. Bourdieu notes the emphasis of elite French schools for

Table 3.1 IBDP English A1 texts studied in 2006

August Strindberg's *Miss Julie* (Sweden)
Henrik Ibsen's *Hedda Gabbler* (Norway)
Federico García Lorca's *House of Bernada Alba* (Spain)
Euripidis's *Medea* (Greece)*
Extracts from:
William Shakespeare's *Twelfth Night* and *King Lear*' (England)
Wole Soyinka's poems (Nigeria)*
Maya Angelou's *I Know Why the Caged Bird Sings* (United States)
War poetry (United Kingdom)
Hermann Hesse's *Siddhartha* (Germany) – WL
Mark Twain's *The Adventures of Huckleberry Finn* (United States)
Roddy Doyle's *Paddy Clarke Ha Ha Ha* (Ireland)
Alice Walker's *The Colour Purple* (United States)*
Alvin Lee and Aaron Pang's *No Other City* (Singapore)
Lu Xun's short stories (China) – WL
Salman Rushdie's *East-West* (India)
Arundhati Roy's *God of Small Things* (India)*

---

* Higher-level texts, WL = world literature text

both written and oral competence and the importance of style as well as content (Bourdieu, 1977; Swartz, 1997); this same emphasis distinguishes the Ace student. In addition to the written papers, the IBDP paper has a strong research and oral communication strand. They have to complete a research paper for Part 1 (World Literature); an Individual Oral Commentary for Part 2 (Detailed Study), timed essays (Paper 1) and an unseen essay (Paper 2) for Part 3 (Groups of Works); and an Individual Oral Presentation for Part 4 (School's Free Choice). In comparison, students offering the A-levels, the equivalent national high-stakes assessment, need only study five texts at the H2 level and are assessed only through a timed written essay (which includes a comparative unseen component) (Singapore Examinations and Assessment Board & Cambridge International Examinations, 2014). The choice of the more rigorous IB paper with its focus on wide reading and varied assessment goes towards crafting a well-read and well-spoken Ace student. Thus, school assessment reinforces students' mastery of the English language and their ability to hold literate conversations about literary and other texts. School practices build on home influences, schooling students in particular ways of thinking and knowing that add to their cultural capital (see Chapter 2 for discussion of students' home resources).

Although the IDBP curriculum is only for Years Five and Six students, the curriculum objectives are filtered down to influence the development of the Years One to Four English syllabus. The syllabus moves from texts from Anglophile countries (*Flowers for Algernon* and *Shakespeare's Merchant of Venice*) in Years One and Two to a postcolonial focus (*Four Continents* and *Poems Deep and Dangerous*) in Years Three and Four to world literature in Years Five and Six. One can see how the text choice deliberately builds up students' understanding of the wider world through this exposure to texts. The alignment between home and school practices is obvious when comparing the boys' home practices to their school practices. The stories read in the classroom came from particular backgrounds and required specific reading practices for the boys to access the meanings in the stories, and their early childhood readings provided a "home advantage" (Lareau, 1989) by contributing to the ease with which they learnt how to read culturally more diverse and difficult texts. That these boys were familiar with Eurocentric texts was echoed by the dean of English when she explained to me that they chose to start with "books that the boys are familiar with before moving on to postcolonial and world literature". Although India and China may be geographically closer, and the poems in the Singaporean anthology *No Other City* (A. Lee & Pang, 2000) are situated in Singapore, for these boys, it was not geographical distance but rather cultural and linguistic distance as well as conceptual difficulty that marked what was easy and what was difficult. The breadth of the IBDP English curriculum expands on the already broad repertoire of books and genres that the students have cultivated through their home and earlier readings.

However, beyond the official curriculum of the school, it is the enacted curriculum (Jackson, 1968) that determines what students actually learn in their classrooms. Through their lessons, the Ace students learn ways of reading and responding to reading that are valued within the school culture. The Ace boys are taught to make "crossings", to become flexible readers who know how to approach different texts with appropriate ways of reading. The case study boys made different kinds of crossings in their everyday reading practices – across different cultures, genres and media – as part of their global-literate identities. Their ability to make these cultural crossings could thus be seen as a learnt process where the school curriculum was scaffolded to help them see across concepts and cultures as they matured. Beyond the actual unfamiliarity of the geographical settings of story worlds, there were hidden cultural codes (R. C. Anderson, 1994) and plural meanings (Barthes, 1974) that the students had to learn to read to understand both the word and the world (Freire, 1991).

The students learnt particular ways of communicating about literary texts and of projecting self as knowledgeable through their lessons and interactions with teachers about texts. The following narrative vignette demonstrates one example of how the students were learning to analyse both literary and popular texts with critical literary lens.

> Jonathan, Gary, Michael and Robert are presenting. Their task is to reflect on the character of Obi in *No Longer at Ease* and the protagonist in a short movie by a Singaporean film-maker, Royston Tan. Jonathan explains that "the girl in

the *New York Girl* (2005) wants to be the first Singaporean girl in Hollywood and Obi wants to change society. Both of them want to break free from stereotypes." At the end of the presentation, Mr. Lee notes that "both characters feel a sense of displacement that is linked to their identities. Obi wants to get rid of the corrupt Nigerian idea but there is a clash when reality differs."

(Field Notes, February 17, 2009)

In the vignette, the students have learnt from their lessons and earlier presentations that it is important to discuss identity and conflict in a literary analysis. This ability to grasp thematic similarities and differences between texts, and to make connections between texts and life, is a literary skill that is carried over into their everyday practices of reading and analysing books that are read institutionally from school. What stands out is the confidence with which they present these abstract ideas and their acquisition of a technical literary language (e.g., "stereotypes"). The teacher builds on their ideas, bringing literary understandings to another level. Students learn vocabulary (e.g., "displacement") and how to further analyse literary texts through Mr. Lee's elaborations after their presentation. Through teacher scaffolding and immersion in the class community of reading (Rex, 2001), the students internalise particular ways of talking about both text and the world, learn that it is all right to analyse texts and the world, and build understandings of self and others through the texts and class focus on postcolonial texts and understanding the other.

These ways of thinking-talking-valuing are internalised and applied to their consumption and conversations about books and other forms of media (Gee, 1996). For example, Sanjeev demonstrates his ability to grasp cultural conflicts in the short stories read in class in the following interview.

I think both of them [the short stories] are to do with the Western side against the traditional side. So I think in *The Only American in Our Village*, the Americans are portrayed slightly negatively, like they are caught up in their own little world that they tend to ignore the others, whereas in *No Longer at Ease* and *The Sacrificial Egg*, the debate is still open. Like the writer feels that both sides are equally important in a sense. But in *The Only American*, it's like Them against Us.

(Interview, March 20, 2009)

Ironically, this familiarity with ways of reading literature in fact led Robert to dismissively remark that the texts read in the Literature classroom were "boring" and that it was easy to do well when one knew what to look out for: "[I]t's almost certain that one will find issues to do with cultural conflict in what we read". This neat, succinct judgement about their study of several short stories in the texts studied for the year (*No Longer at Ease* by Chinua Achebe and *Four Continents*, a postcolonial anthology of short stories) reveals their internalisation of a particular way of thinking about the world that facilitated their literary and worldly access. These ways of thinking and talking about texts were not limited to school readings but were part and parcel of their daily talk and writing about books.

The students were also schooled in particular ways of thinking privileged by the assessment system. Unable to complete every scene in *Macbeth* in time for the examination, the selected drama text for Year Four, Ms. Rani confessed that she had to resort to teaching key scenes and prioritising the skills of close reading and oral commentary, which was how *Macbeth* was to be assessed. In class, she taught the students to close read key scenes and encouraged them to make connections between the scenes, emphasising the importance of making thematic links and conducting complex character analysis and the need to use textual evidence to support the analysis. Even in elite schools, the examination-oriented culture of Singapore influences how teachers determine teaching priorities. Yet, the very fact that the assessment focused on oral assessment expanded the scope of classroom lessons and teacher expectations for what an Ace Institution student needed to demonstrate to show linguistic and literary competence. The oral component required students to closely analyse a selected text and to spend eight minutes explaining their analysis to the examiner. This was followed by a question and answer session. This constant emphasis on oral communication and literary analysis was evident across both Mr. Lee and Ms. Rani's classes, and the constant reiteration and practice helped facilitated students' understanding of literary texts, ways of talking about text, and verbal dexterity. Moreover, in addition to the core curriculum, compulsory oral communication modules, annual inter-class debates and oratorical competitions contributed to the general sense that success in oral communication was essential.

Students learnt to demonstrate literary competence in class. For example, although Michael professed indifference to schoolwork, he participated selectively in classroom discussions and handed in A essays. The following conversation was observed during a routine lesson on *Macbeth*, where Michael volunteers his analysis of the main character of Macbeth.

Michael: His "vaulting ambition" clouded his judgment.
Ms. Rani: He lost his morality in the process.
Michael: The fact that his ambition was so great . . .
Ms. Rani: Exactly, in the end, the tables turned, and Macbeth rather than Lady Macbeth becomes the domineering one.
Michael: Now you know who is wearing the pants.

(Field Notes, April 21, 2009)

In this quick-fire exchange with Ms. Rani, Michael demonstrated quick thinking, deft textual analysis, and a witty sense of humour with his wordplay on gender roles ("Now you know who is wearing the pants"). What is more striking in this exchange is the equal role assumed by teacher and student discussing *Macbeth*. The confidence with which Michael parries with Ms. Rani reveals his confident assurance of his knowledge of the text and of his opinions. This confidence the boys had in their evaluation about books is carried across to their interaction with me, the adult researcher: They wrote long email reflections on their reading practices and were generally willing to share their opinions about books with me, even without prompting. They would recommend books to me and share their uncensored opinion of the text or lesson as I sat in class for lesson observations over the year. The cultural knowledge, English fluency and verbal dexterity of the Ace Institution boys constitute part of the Ace boy's global-literate identity.

Critical distinctions and tactical readings: Ace boys' cultural knowledge and dispositions

The construction of the global-literate identity in the form of cultural knowledge is a process that begins at home rather than school. Bourdieu notes that the elite students' cultural and linguistic competence is the result of

> . . . unintentional learning made possible by a disposition acquired through domestic or scholastic inculcation of legitimate culture. This transposable disposition, armed with a set of perceptual and evaluative schemes that are available for general application, inclines its owner towards other cultural experiences and enables him to perceive, classify and memorize them differently.
>
> (Bourdieu, 1984, p. 28)

In Chapter Two, I examined how the boys learn particular ways of thinking about books through home and earlier schooling experiences. They learn to respond personally and confidently to books and to evaluate books critically in their everyday practices of reading. Lareau (2003) noted in her book, *Unequal Childhoods*, that middle-class children learn to address adults as equals, to expect to have their opinions accepted and to learn to negotiate through language. In the same way, the boys in the study had developed a way of talking about books that they apply to texts read for school and for pleasure. They do not perceive books and knowledge as pure scholastic knowledge irrelevant to their lived worlds; rather, they learn to apply the knowledge learnt in books, and their knowledge about the world of books, to their response to and evaluation of books. They were at ease with talking to others about books and their relation to the world around them.

In the earlier section of this chapter, I explained how the official and enacted curriculum of the school cultivates a form of worldly knowledge. These institutional habitus and practices of distinction are supported by students' home-acquired ways of reading. Used to a culture of wide and adventurous reading, the boys were confident readers who were unafraid to recommend books to me during the course of the study. This confidence in their reading tastes was a form of distinction that placed them above the masses. Through habits inculcated from a young age, they are plugged into global book markets through informal institutions such as chain bookstores Borders (defunct since 2011) and Books Kinokuniya as well as institutionalised book markets through their school readings. As such, book consumption was very much part of their identities, and their knowledge of books provided them with the confidence with which to evaluate their readings and the reading practices of others. They read both popular and classic literature, and this cultural omnivorousness in English books was further expanded by the school's prescribed world literature texts and reading lists.

The confidence in books is evident in the way they evaluated books. The boys evaluated books from two different criteria – *aesthetic value* (literary value) and *entertainment value* (popular value) – and positioned themselves as competent readers who were able to evaluate their readings and make informed reading choices. In the following excerpt, Sanjeev positioned himself as someone who was aware of the quality of available choices, even if he did not always read what he considered valuable.

Chin: Why do you like Dan Brown?
Michael: Damn nice. The mystery is very cool.
Sanjeev: (interjecting) I read in Primary 6, and I thought it was damn good. Then, after that, a few months later, I realized it's –
Michael: (adamantly) It's damn GOOD!
Sanjeev: No, as in, it's damn entertaining but it's not good.

(Group Interview, February 6, 2009)

Sanjeev appealed to the dual criteria of entertainment and aesthetic value to evaluate Dan Brown's novels but ultimately seemed to indicate that the worth of one's reading should be judged by aesthetic rather than entertainment value. Though he admitted to reading "trashy novels" when he did not "feel like reading anything too heavy", he was quick to criticise such books from an ironic distance (Ang, 1982). By being able to identify the "trashy" nature of the book, Sanjeev positioned himself as someone with taste – who could distinguish what was good and what was not but who also allowed himself the occasional indulgence of reading "trashy books", that which was worthless from an aesthetic angle but appealed to the popular masses. Despite Michael's vehement objections to Sanjeev's categorisation of Dan Brown, Michael too was a flexible reader who could access both popular and prize-winning literature.

Critical readings of texts are aligned with school displays of literary competence. Yet, these boys have so imbibed the values of literariness that it is displayed in their daily talk and discussion about texts. Robert, in an email reading log, conveyed his opinion of the "simply awesome" *A Hat Full of Sky* by Terry Pratchett.

> Under the humor and satire lies a theme of self-acceptance and confidence, and the main character, Tiffany is rather like me, or many others of my peers, I'm afraid: Inquisitive, and perhaps looked down upon by elders, yet possessed of a unique character. It's rare that I find a character that I really can relate to, but Terry Pratchett does it so effortlessly it's almost disturbing in its accuracy.
>
> (February 2, 2009)

In this evaluation, Robert identified the literary genre ("satire") and stated the theme of the book ("theme of self-acceptance and confidence") with easy confidence. In his email, he neatly combines a reader response approach (Rosenblatt, 1994), to a critical textual character analysis in line with New Criticism's emphasis on the text (Brooks, 1947; Richards, 1929). This critical analysis is applied not just to print texts but also to other genres and modes. In another example, Robert competently contrasts the key ideas of *Wicked*, the musical and the novel by Gregory Maguire.

> The musical is more or less based around the friendship as opposed to the whole underlying story of Elphaba in the book. In the book, you have Elphaba portrayed as this demon child at birth, with fangs and all but you don't see it in the musical because it is not really important, in a sense, to the whole message of friendship and stuff. . . . The majority of the musical is about friendship and all. Relationships. It [Elphaba trying to save the animals] figures as a plot device.
> (February 27, 2009)

The comparison requires the understanding of musical and book conventions and how certain elements are presented because of the chosen mode of presentation. What stands out again is Robert's confidence in sharing his own opinion. Here, one can again see how the boys' out-of-school readings and discussions of books resemble school-required ways of talking about texts.

The boys' confidence in critiquing texts was not limited to their own reading but extend to their critical evaluation of schools readings.

Robert: The thing with all these award-winning books is that . . . sometimes I think that the people who give literature prizes don't want to be entertained.
Joshua: [laughs] They're the super-artsy people who have very weird taste.
Robert: Who appreciate minimalist plays and such.
(Group Interview, May 26, 2009)

In this open critique of the school's curriculum choices, Robert and Joshua juxtaposed the concept of entertainment for the masses against award-winning books that do not appeal to the masses. Robert's comment about people "who appreciate minimalist plays and such" was in direct reference to his drama club teacher, who had wanted to put up a minimalist play for a national drama competition. Robert was familiar with literary styles and genres, knew about high culture and had the terms to talk about it, even if he scoffed at it. This criticality was a form of distinction for him; he felt confident enough of his knowledge of different kinds of works to critique the school's choices.

The boys' familiarity with books was what entitled them to criticise the books and critique what they and others read from an ironic distance. Ien Ang (1982), in her study of soap opera viewers, has pointed out that what distinguishes readers and viewers is the ability to take an ironic viewing attitude towards mass culture, where the reader is able to distance himself or herself to critique the soap opera. These boys were able to read high and popular culture and were confident about their own reading choices. They were able to evaluate the kinds of books they read and categorise them as either literary or popular and to confidently label themselves as particular kinds of readers in relation to what others read. Distinction for these boys laid not so much in the books they read but in their confidence and their flexible ability to access different kinds of texts and make critical evaluations of these readings. Both personal and institutional habitus cohere to construct critical attitudes towards texts. The wide reading obtained in their home and early schooling years ensured success in their engagement with literary texts from all over the world. The ability to cross various genres and texts is part of the boys' identities and attributed to them as natural "style". Their distinction lies not just in being able to read different texts but to read them critically with traditional school-preferred lenses. This internalisation of critical reading, and the ability to talk and write about them in highly literate language, demonstrates how traditional literacies continue to be important despite seeming democratisation with new technologies and multimodal forms of communication (Warshauer, 2007). The ability and confidence to evaluate critically, inscribed on the boys' reading and thinking, is a critical factor for success at school and knowledge-intensive work.

Rather than marking elite status solely by what is consumed, elites distinguish themselves by the way they appreciate and critique culture. Khan (2012) observes in his St. Paul's study that

> [W]hat marks elites as elites is not a singular point of view or purpose but rather their capacity to pick and choose, combine and consume a wide gamut of the social strata. The highbrow snob is almost dead. In his place is a cosmopolitan elite that freely consumes high and low culture, and everything in between. The new adolescent elite listens to classical and to rap; they eat at fine restaurants and at diners. They are at ease everywhere in the world.
> (p. 115)

Ways of consuming (including the consumption of texts) are thus forms of embodied cultural capital, inscribed on the body of the elite student who is at ease with the world. Cultural knowledge and critical consumption mark the elite student as globally literate. The knowledge, skills and dispositions are translated into particular ways of talking and writing about texts. These students move with ease between school and home practices of reading.

On the other hand, whereas the boys may be critical of school readings, they are tactical in their adherence to school-required ways of reading. The ability to play the game or to move with ease within institutional structures is one mark of middle-class upbringing (Demerath, 2009; Lareau, 2003). The boys in the study played the game in their school readings, choosing to comply with institutional demands of reading while resisting school readings in other ways. For example, although Robert thought that the school choice of texts were boring, he had to "grin and bear it" because he wanted to do well academically. Similarly, Michael professed indifference to his readings but made sure that he did well on his school tests. The boys thus complied with school norms of literacy through classroom participation, written work and oral presentations that formed the modes of assessment for literary competence.

De Certeau's (1984) concept of "tactics" and "strategies" highlights the flexible practices of these boys in their relation to school literature. For de Certeau, many everyday practices are tactical in character. Strategies are moves that are situated in "proper" places and can be linked to institutional relations. On the other hand, tactics are disassociated from institutions and describe the improvisational aspect of practice. The act of reading is tactical in nature, where a reader "insinuates into another person's text the ruses of pleasure and appropriation"(1984, p. xxi), choosing to read the text as and when he pleases and seizing opportunities to read into the text what the author did not mean. On the other hand, school-sanctioned ways of reading can thus be viewed as approved strategic moves where readers are encouraged to view the status of a text as well as what the text is trying to say in institutionally-approved ways. Although these boys had to read and write in accordance with school-sanctioned ways of reading, they also chose to read these texts with the twin lenses of school-derived aesthetic criteria and the mass consumption criteria of entertainment.

Like Willis's (1975) working-class lads in the Britain of the 1970s, these boys resisted school culture in their critique of school readings, but unlike the lads, they actually believed in the relative value of the study of literature and were willing to comply with institutional norms that they saw as having tangible and intangible benefits in their acquisition of a globally-valued literacy. These observations are in line with Reay's observations that middle-class boys had "less to contest" because "they are served by a curriculum and system aligned with their capitals and interests" (Reay, 2006a, p. 344). Yet, complicatedly, they did not just see reading literature as a means to a good grade and better educational opportunity. They enjoyed the subject, even though they may not see how it could contribute directly to future educational endeavours. Thus, Sanjeev, who planned to pursue an MBA degree in an Ivy League university, admitted that he "liked literature" and that it helped hone his analytical and language skills and his "understanding of human nature". Yet, he also made special effort to work on his writing and improve his grades so that he could acquire a literary identity that was awarded with A essays by the end of the year.

The ability to make these tactical moves was part of the boys' flexible manoeuvring in the construction of their identities as global-literate citizens able to plug into different forms of literacies appropriately. The ability to read different kinds of texts for different purposes and to know when and how to apply these readings was a form of intercultural capital that they were unconscious of but utilised accordingly. Intercultural capital is a "type of social and cultural capital that comprises the experiences, dispositions, knowledge and understandings of an individual that result from interactions with others in intercultural context" (Tobin, Kincheloe, & Patron, 2012, p. 63). Luke and Goldstein (2006), in their discussion of the cosmopolitan teacher, suggest that this form of intercultural capital requires deep cultural understanding of others and of difference. Intercultural capital "is the capacity to engage in acts of knowledge, power and exchange across space divides and social geographies, across diverse communities, populations and epistemic stances" (Luke, 2004, p. 1429). On a superficial level, it is clear that the boys' linguistic and cultural flexibility is a form of intercultural capital that holds value across different cultures and markets. As tactical readers, they are able to plug into different knowledge forms, including those that have symbolic value and potential economic value in portraying them as highly literate individuals within and beyond the Singapore context.

However, it is uncertain if the boys have developed a deep understanding of the other or of difference through the texts studied and the "critical" ways of reading in the class. In a paper elsewhere, I have discussed how the boys demonstrate little understanding that their reading habits and academic excellence are partly the result of their privilege. Instead, they choose to see others' lack of success as a result of lack of personal ambition and effort and their success as a result of their hard work (Loh, 2016a). Interestingly, Tan's (2004) survey on social stratification and orientation revealed that middle- and upper-income Singaporeans tended to attribute their success to hard work, whereas those from lower classes tended to attribute success to luck. Although the aim of exposing students to world literature is to get students to see beyond their parochial view of the world to a truly cosmopolitan view that is aware of the cultural complexity of the other, it is questionable whether all the students imbibed this worldview or if they just cultivate a "superficial multiculturalism" (Resnik, 2008) with surface awareness of other cultures through their readings. This superficial multiculturalism provided by the cultural capital of the world literature curriculum positions them as ideal global workers able to get along with multicultural others in the same social circles but may not increase their awareness to others who do not share the same social circumstances within the nation and the world (Loh, 2012, 2016a).

Developing a global literate identity, meritocracy and pedagogical equity?

The school curriculum is not neutral knowledge, and what counts as legitimated knowledge on the official curriculum is the result of complex struggles and compromises among several groups in society (Apple, 1990, 1992; Applebee, 1974; Kliebard, 2004; Luke, 1988). Within Singapore, education is driven by the necessity of economics, resulting in an efficient distribution of educational resources to meet the economic needs of the country. Elite students, exempted from having to rigidly follow the official MOE syllabus and take the high-stakes national examinations, are in fact more than fulfilling the national desire to go global through their construction of global-literate selves through schooled practices of reading. For the Ace Institution students at least, the IBDP certification is another route to global mobility. In addition, the dispositions of wide reading, oral and written fluency, and research skills picked up during the course of study prepare them to work in global contexts.

The boys' possession of knowledge in the form of English school classics, more recent postcolonial works, world literature and their knowledge of contemporary, prize-winning and popular literature is a form of cultural capital. More importantly, their ability to consume widely and their ability to use these texts appropriately is a form of intercultural capital as they were able to access knowledge that was relevant for different contexts. It is their relation to knowledge – their ability to utilise such knowledge in appropriate situations – that puts them in a position of power. Their access to linguistically and culturally sophisticated texts and flexible ways of reading are facilitated by their head start in accessing varied texts and ways of reading from a young age, whether through the attention of their parents or through attending enrichment classes. Their discursive practices and approach to literary reading are further developed through school curriculum and instructional practices of reading and assessment. As a result, they acquire a firm grasp of language and texts though their home and school readings and ways of reading, demonstrating flexible literate selves relevant to global English-speaking markets. They know when to use these moves and to shift between modes of reading for school purpose and for their own purpose. Their flexibility is a form of power that allows them to plug into global notions of literacy relevant to international markets in their localised context. These expectations for higher standards of linguistic competence and literary knowledge for elite students are forms of linguistic and cultural capital that distinguish elite students and are built into the national habitus of distinction for Singaporeans whose English will be "no different from the best in English speaking countries". Though there is no clear mandate that these top students will only come from elite schools, institutional habitus cohere with home backgrounds to favour such students.

The students are in fact part of the nation's plan for a "strategic cosmopolitanism" which prioritises the cognitive value of English language and downplays the aesthetic value of English by relegating Literature to an optional subject at upper secondary (Choo, 2014). However, as the case study of the Ace boys demonstrates, their socialisation into reading includes the acquisition of knowledge (of literary texts) and dispositions (ways of thinking about, talking about and writing about these texts and other texts) marks them as different from other students accustomed to functional, skills-based approaches towards reading. This focus on the functional is embedded in the official curriculum as well as practices of teaching (Kramer-Dahl, 2007; R. Silver et al., 2013), with the MOE syllabus focusing the six skills of listening, reading, viewing, speaking, writing and representing and on grammar and vocabulary (Ministry of Education, 2012). This approach is in line with a cognitively-oriented and instrumental approach to critical thinking (Koh, 2013), which assumes thinking is a set of skills that can be taught in isolation from issues and values. However, there is a tendency within a skills-oriented curriculum for teachers to neglect to teach students the kinds of content or information that are required to make knowledge meaningful in a global world. Moreover, all too often, teachers' beliefs that students must acquire a basic literacy before being allowed to engaged in critical discussion of texts and topics limit the teaching and learning in English classrooms (Albright, Kramer-Dahl, & Kwek, 2008; Hogan, 2010; Kramer-Dahl & Kwek, 2011).

Anyon's (1980) work on social class and curriculum has shown how work tasks and interactions may differ in social class communities, based on assumptions about students' event roles in the working world. In her ethnographic study of five contrasting elementary schools in the United States, she noted that children in a working-class school are exposed to routine and mechanical work in school, reflective of their future labour. Children in a middle-class school learn to give the right answers and comply with authority, which prepares them for bureaucratic work. Children at the affluent business school are encouraged to acquire symbolic capital in the form of linguistic, artistic, and scientific expression and encouraged to be creative, preparing them for future innovation and production work. Finally, children at the executive elite school are given "knowledge of and practice in manipulating the socially legitimated tools of analysis of systems" (p. 89) which they can eventually use to manage the production of systems. Although the curricular, pedagogical and evaluation practices of schools may not be so clearly defined, as suggested by Anyon, certainly her point that students may be restricted to particular forms of knowledge and learning based on their access to particular kinds of schools is valid. The "hidden curriculum of work" at school influences the attitudes of administrators and teachers and results in differentiated curriculum, pedagogy and evaluation that students receive.

This "hidden curriculum" (Anyon, 1980; Jackson, 1968) in Singapore is evident in the enacted curriculum of schools. In the examination-oriented, teacher-centred pedagogical culture in mainstream Singapore schools (Albright & Kramer-Dahl, 2009; Curdt-Christiansen & Silver, 2012; Kramer-Dahl, 2007), a *worksheet* pedagogy which emphasises giving the right answers and filling in the blanks often persists in classrooms, contrary to official policy to encourage critical and creative thinking (Ministry of Education, 2010). In contrast, elite schools that do not have to adhere to the national curriculum may provide more opportunities for *inquiry-based* pedagogy, with programmes and lessons designed to encourage critical and creative thinking. This differentiation in education is also evident in the social studies curriculum, where students are allocated three distinct roles: (1) cosmopolitan elite leaders; (2) globally-oriented but locally-rooted mid-level executives and workers; and (3) local 'heartlander' followers, sorted by the educational tracks they are streamed into (L.-C. Ho, 2012). In relation to the critical thinking curriculum, Lim (2014) argues that the construction of critical thinking as a course available only to A-level students who are bound for university degrees excludes other students from the kind of rational, abstract and utilitarian thinking that is seen as being within the purview of a selected few. This allows for the reproduction of a "new middle class, who are able to convert their skills at problem solving, management, systems engineering . . . into broader forms of symbolic and cultural capital, heightening their status as a group in society" (p. 72). The construction of global-literate citizens ready to plug into global and national markets requires national effort, and the habitus of meritocracy and equal opportunity supports the sorting of citizens for different functions and markets.

In this chapter, I have focused on how the boys cultivate global-literate identities, supported by school habitus aligned with national habitus. Social class contributes to the boys' acquisition of proficient English language skills and flexible literacies appropriate for global markets. Rather than celebrating the agency and achievements of the Ace boys as "shape-shifting portfolio" individuals (Gee, 2004), it is essential to complicate the problematic issue of literacy acquisition by pointing out that the availability of rich resources and networks for middle-class students do contribute to the construction of reading identities that align with school-sanctioned literacies and perceived global-mindedness. The richness of the resources that allowed the boys to construct identities as global-literate citizens highlights the lack of others, and educators need to ask how meritocratic literacy education can take place when some children are better prepared than others for flexibility from early childhood. Given the different starting points and constraints for different populations in individual systems, how can flexible literacies be understood and framed to prepare students for a globalised world? What kinds of skills, content and thinking are expected for *all* students when it comes to reading and language learning? What is the role of literature study in the national context?

One approach in the United States has been that of creating a list of words and phrases to capture the core knowledge required to boost the "cultural literacy" of students (Hirsch, 1987). This may make up for cultural knowledge but does not contribute to the accumulation of experiences or dispositions towards knowledge. At the end of the day, learning to be a flexible reader requires agile and appropriate responses to a wide variety of texts. Taking a linear and functional approach of language learning as an "objective", decontextualised, skills-based subject neglects the notion that language learning is a values-laden and disposition-oriented endeavour. At the policy level, there needs to be a fundamental re-evaluation of the skills-only approach so as to question what kinds of issues students need to be exposed to in the English classroom to become critical and innovative, civic-minded, globally-aware, multicultural national and world citizens – an aim captured in the 21st Century Competencies Framework (Ministry of Education, 2015). Critical, place-based pedagogies can be designed to encourage inquiry-based learning about meaningful national and global issues and serve as bridges to the academic literacies that are necessary for educational advancement (Comber, 2016; Luke & Carrington, 2004). How the English curriculum can address "issues which may resonate locally but which have global implications" so that students can develop a "global critical English" (Wallace, 2003, p. 97) is an important consideration for future revisions of the syllabus or curriculum guidelines.

4 *Levelling* the reading gap
Socio-spatial perspectives

In this chapter, I turn to socio-spatial perspectives to understand how the distribution and organisation of space may influence everyday practices of reading and contribute to or inhibit the kinds of learning desired. Here, I look to space to extend the concept of practice by examining how spatialising practice can generate new ways of understanding access and barriers to learning to read within the institutional and physical space of school. Whereas much reading research and instruction focuses on curriculum and instruction, the space within which learning takes place tends to be neglected. Space differs from place, which is bounded (Cresswell, 2015). A place is a "meaningful location" which includes the location, the locale (the material setting for social relations including buildings and gardens) and a sense of place or an emotional attachment to place (Agnew, 1987). Space, on the other hand, is a more abstract concept (Cresswell, 2015) consisting of networks and flows that move across and influence what happens in bounded space.

Spatial perspectives require the understanding that schools are not static, bounded containers; instead, they constitute a network of national, institutional and community discourses that evolve over historical time and across space (Nespor, 1997), and these practices have an impact on the social relations and practices of students and other actors within the space. The spatial emphasis highlights that "students and parents are not just traversing 'empty space', they are actively engaged in constituting, and being constituted by, spaces and places" (Gulson, 2007, p. 5 in Mills & Comber, 2015). Learning to read is thus not only a mechanical process of understanding how the letters on a page come together to create words and paragraphs but involves one's relation to space and other individuals within the space. At the core of this analysis is the notion that a critical spatial justice, "an intentional and focused emphasis on the spatial or geographical aspects of justice and injustice" (Soja, 2009, p. 2), can make visible hidden structures that lead to uneven access to educational resources and opportunities. Attending to the dominant discourses in the space of school through the lens of social class alerts educators to differentiation, the ideologies underlying this differentiation and how differentiation may work out in practice to reproduce inequalities. Taking a spatial perspective acts as a counterpoint to deficit notions (Valencia, 2010) of the students as readers; rather than focusing on the *student-as-problem* (reluctant readers, poor readers and struggling readers), zooming in on space or *structure-as-problem* allows for contextualised and nuanced understandings of how systemic issues may hinder desired student learning. The built and lived environment of a school may perpetuate constraints to learning. Given that the school is a dominant institution for the reproduction and transformation of existing inequities, applying a critical spatial lens is a deliberate attempt to move beyond the individual student to identify possibilities for intervention at a structural level.

To understand the space of practice for reading, I zoom in on the comparative spaces of Ace and Tembusu school libraries as micro-ecosystems within which to understand how reading is perceived and enacted within the schools. The space of the school library, typically associated with the cultivation of reading habits (Adkins & Brendler, 2015; Krashen, 2004; McKechnie & Rothbauer, 2006), provides a bounded space in the schooling context within which to understand how reading identities and habits may or may not in fact be encouraged in particular schooling contexts. It may even serve as a space for differentiated education for students from different socioeconomic backgrounds when access to resources and learning within both the home and school are uneven.

The space of practice within which literacy is perceived, enacted and lived is thus a political space with potential for the reproduction as well as transformation of power relations, and literacy research must take into account how differentiated space can reproduce and even exacerbate existing inequities, despite the best intentions of educators. Acknowledgement of the realities of lived space is one way to reimagine space and to transform present and future space by opening up alternative views of the world as it is (Massey, 2005).

Spatial practice, reading and the role of school libraries

In David Harvey's (2009) *Social Justice and the City*, he argues that social practices and processes influence space, which in turn further constrain or enable other social practices. Space is different from place in not being bounded, in not being container-like, and consists of not just the material but also imagined spaces (Leander, Phillips, & Taylor, 2010; Lefebvre, 1991; Massey, 2005; Soja, 2009) that permeate the actual contained space that is under scrutiny. Spatialising practice foregrounds how everyday practices are permeated by dominant ideological discourses and questions the uncritical acceptance of taken-for-granted and often routine reading practices present in schools. Doreen Massey (2005) calls for an intentional reworking of the dominant discourses of particular spaces to reimagine possibilities for change. Recognising that space is often perceived as hegemonic and static but yet refusing to see space as constructed by a single master narrative opens up space for other stories and for unearthing assumptions that underlie the way we think and act within specific contexts and how that space governs social relations.

Understanding space as ideologically interconnected space that can constrain or enable *ways of doing-thinking-doing-feeling-being* makes visible the multiple, interrelated discourses governing space and its imposition on individuals occupying that space. Lefebvre (1991) explains that through spatial practice, social relations are reproduced or transformed. Spatial arrangements mediate social relations, and the way space is used and organised signifies the importance of particular spaces and the social relations within that space.

> Everybody knows what is meant when we speak of a 'room' in an apartment, the 'corner' of the street, a 'marketplace', a shopping or cultural 'centre', a public 'place', and so on. *These terms of everyday discourse serve to distinguish, but not to isolate, particular spaces, and in general to describe a social space. They correspond to a specific use of that space, and hence to a spatial practice that they express and constitute.* Their interrelations are ordered in a specific way. Might it not be a good idea, therefore, first to make an inventory of them, and then to try and ascertain what paradigm gives them their meaning, what syntax governs their organization?
>
> (Lefebvre, 1991, p. 16, *italics mine*)

The spatial practice that Lefebvre speaks of is the everyday quotidian lived experiences of individuals, which are ordered by competing ideologies and discourses permeating the space. By closely observing spatial practice, practicing what de Certeau (1984) terms walking the city – tracking the rhythms and cycles of place, observing occupied and empty spaces, attending to use and isolation and noting habitual movements – it is possible to observe how social relations are shaped by underlying and competing discourses within each societal space. Within the Singapore context, the dominant discourses of meritocracy and equal opportunity govern the logic of educational policy and filter down to educational practice in the form of excessive competition and desire to excel; at the same time, competing discourses such as character education, nurturing the child, and student-centred learning compete for recognition and acceptance. It is only through attention to spatial practice, to how these discourses are worked out in the everyday, that one can begin to discern which discourses are valued and how they are valued and worked out in the day-to-day operation and experience of schools and individuals.

That individuals constitute and are constituted by space is evident in Foucault's (1995) well-known discussion of the panopticon in *Discipline and Punish*. In his description of the prison design, he shows how unequal power relations are entrenched in the layout of the prison with the tower in the centre according the guard the power of observation from a higher vantage point. Prisoners below, unable to see the guards, behave under the threat of surveillance. The very design of the prison locates power in the prison guard and determines the relationship between the all-seeing guard and the subordinate prisoners. Space, mediated by influential individuals and institutions, thus serves hegemonic interests by maintaining unequal social relations through perception and organisation of space (Lefebvre, 1991). Hegemony requires a certain *doxa*, experience that makes "the natural and social world appear self-evident" (Bourdieu, 1977, p. 164), and individuals' unquestioning habitual use of space sediments ways of thinking and moving about the world.

Dominant views of what kinds of learning count and how learning should occur are lived out in the design and organisation of schools. The traditional classroom design with the teacher situated in front of rows of students (resembling Foucault's panopticon) maximises supervision and surveillance, and emphasises the dutiful banking (Freire, 1970) of knowledge into the minds of passive students through textbooks, lectures and teacher-centred lessons (Nair, Fielding, & Lackney, 2009). In their work on Western school buildings, Grosvenor and Burke (2008) point out that from the introduction of mass schooling in the 19th century to more contemporary times, there has been a marked anxiety about the control and discipline of students.

> Anxieties about the control and disciplining of large numbers of individuals, both children and adults, within the institution are reflected through discussions about the arrangement of classrooms, corridors, stairwells, gates and fences, and latterly, the installation and positioning of security cameras. The opening to the wider community has conflicted with anxieties about risk and the provision of a safe haven for children, and school buildings have altered considerably over time in response to health and safety regulations.
> (pp. 21–22)

The design and organisation of educational space is thus very much tied to dominant ideologies about schooling, and the kinds of schools, buildings, classrooms and common spaces reveal much about a community's vision or limitation for its educational future (Grosvenor & Burke, 2008).

Within Singapore, the traditional model of the classroom dominated Singapore classrooms in the 1980s, when teacher-centric approaches were common. In a Singapore education report to UNESCO, it was stated that

> [a]s teaching methods of the conventional or traditional style (i.e. teacher-centric approach) are prevalent in Singapore schools, and as the progressive or non-formal style of teaching have yet to prove their superiority, the design of classrooms closely follow the traditional model.
>
> Teaching aids used in classrooms include chalkboards, overhead projectors, maps, charts and the like. The design of the classroom has to provide the appropriate facilities for these aides, including adequate storage space.
> (Liew, 1981, pp. 27–28)

The traditional classroom format continues to dominate Singapore classrooms, despite shifts towards student-centred and collaborative learning, and the use of technology. This illustrates how ideas of teaching and learning are underpinned by the way classrooms are structured and can affect how learning happens and vice versa.

Schools as social spaces thus govern social relations among individuals and the relations among individuals and society. Just as each city and community produces its own space, according to its own rules with an internal logic dictated by social relations, and influences social relations (Lefebvre, 1991), the organisation of social spaces in schools governs the relationships between teachers and students, students and students, and students and the school. A common-sense logic of organisation may not bear up to scrutiny, and what may seem like an inclusive space to some may be viewed as exclusive, depending on one's position in the field of power. In Schmidt's (2015) study of school space, she demonstrated that the universally regarded "safe" place of school may serve as places of both inclusion and exclusion. For minority youth in her study who were identified as lesbian, gay, bisexual and queer (LGBQ), there were limited safe spaces within the school where they could mingle and be seen. Attending to who has access to space and how spaces are accessed can reveal unequal power relations within the space of school. Youths from different backgrounds respond to different school spaces differently: In Khan's (2012) study of the elite students at his alma mater, St. Pauls', he observes that although the affluent youths fit in easily with the expectations and culture of the school, some of the less privileged youths struggle and learn to cope by "acting". Those with the "right" dispositions negotiate the elite school without effort in contrast to those who have to learn how to blend in with the crowd.

By attending to students' actual use and experience of the space of two contrasting school libraries, this chapter makes clear who and what is included and excluded in each library and examines how they are included or excluded. Furthermore, focusing on the use of space through detailed observations, in tandem with conversations with the students as users, can provide insight into *actual* (cf. perceived) use of space. In a study on the space of school libraries, Shilling and Cousins (1990) demonstrated how understanding the (mis) alignment between students' and authorities' perceptions and uses of space can provide insight into why students associate themselves with or disassociate themselves from the use of the school library. They showed how students may use the library in ways unintended by official authorities and how official regulation and unofficial colonisation of the social space may exclude certain student populations from using the library.

The experience of space is affective and involves emotional response to space (Tuan, 1974). In Margaret Meek's *Learning to Read* (1982), her description of how to introduce books and reading to young children is permeated with references to the emotional and spatial connections between books and the experience of reading with the adult as mediator of the reading experience.

> The best reason for introducing books to children is that you enjoy books and want to share your pleasure in them. Do you like stories? Do you enjoy songs, poems, rhymes, and jokes? If you do any of these things, then look for a book you think you might enjoy reading with your child. Trust your own judgement to choose it, or borrow one from a library after you have had a

browse around in the children's picture book section. Sit, relaxed, with the child on your knee, and read the story with pleasure he can feel and share. If the experience is a good one, repeat it sometime later and see what happens.

(p. 29)

Undoubtedly, Meek's instruction assumes a reading parent who might have little difficulty choosing a book he or she is interested in. It does not quite take into account the uninterested or uneducated parent who might be willing but not sufficiently competent to model a pleasurable reading experience. What stands out, however, is the reference to the emotional connection to particular kinds of books the adults enjoy and to places and actions, such as sitting in a relaxed position with the child on the knee. In an exploration of the pleasurable reading experiences of Singaporeans, examining the memories documented in the *Singapore Memory Project*, a community project by the National Library Board to capture Singaporean's memories of events, places and people, I observed that the accounts of memorable reading experiences often included emotional responses to places, books and people (Loh, 2016a). Pleasurable experiences with reading are often experienced by the good readers in Chapter 3. When adolescent readers see value in reading and identify with it, they are more likely to engage in reading activities (F. Smith, 1988). Middle-class children with access to rich physical resources are more likely to pick up positive emotional responses to places such as libraries and bookstores and experiences of reading due to their constant exposure to and positive experiences with reading and reading spaces. This identification with reading encourages them to seek more experiences related to reading.

School spaces can also provide alternative spaces to encourage a social life around books and reading to replicate pleasurable experiences of reading. Examining how space is lived in practice through minute attention to the lived space helps educators to trace the detailed daily use of an individual's responses to space. In so doing, an awareness of the (mis)alignment between ideal and practice may be brought to the foreground. This in turn allows one to see how ideology and power relations may govern the use of particular places and contribute to ineffective as well as inequitable practices. From this awareness or praxis (Freire, 1970), social transformation becomes possible.

The space of school libraries and reading

The importance placed on the school library as a key node in raising the reading and academic achievement of students is well-supported by research documenting the role of school libraries in supporting reading scores and academic achievement (Barratt, 2010; Lance, 2002; Lance & Hofshire, 2012; Todd & Kuhlthau, 2005). This faith in the power of school libraries is evidenced in the L!brary initiative in New York by the Robin Hood Foundation to work with schools in high-poverty neighbourhoods with low academic achievement to transform their school libraries into vital resources for the school community in the hope that it will impact and contribute to improved student performance (Robin Hood, n.d.); 62 school libraries in New York have been transformed since 2002. Extensive reading is correlated to academic achievement (Krashen, 2004), and effective school libraries can do much to support a reading culture (Adkins & Brendler, 2015; Makatche & Oberlin, 2011; Wejrowski & McRae, 2013). Libraries and school libraries can play key roles in supporting educational structures by motivating students to read through the provision of a variety of materials, providing a supportive environment for literacy and reading conversations and encouraging student autonomy in making their reading choices (Adkins & Brendler, 2015).

From a socio-spatial perspective, attending to the school library and how it contributes to the cultivation of a reading culture in school can be seen as an issue of equitable access. Harvey (2009) argues that much of the dominant discourse of urban planning, driven by the profit aims of capitalism and efficiency, often aggravates social divides and exacerbates social inequities. He argues that although need is seen as relative, there are basic needs, such as food, housing, transport and medical facilities, and education that should be made available to all. For Harvey, urban planning should not just attend to the management of resources; rather, there should be attention given to how to ensure a just distribution of resources. What counts as just distribution needs to be established within the community and experts in the field, and an equitable distribution must take care not to exclude or marginalise some within the community. For Harvey, a sense of territorial justice is when

1 The distribution of income should be such that (a) the needs of the population within each territory are met, (b) resources are so allocated to maximize interritorial multiplier effects, and (c) extra resources are allocated to help overcome special difficulties stemming from the physical and social environment.
2 The mechanisms (institutional, organizational, political and economic) should be such that the prospects of the least advantaged territory are as great as they possibly can be.

(pp. 116–117)

In other words, care must be taken to ensure that education as a public good is accessible to all, and more should be invested into ensuring that the disadvantaged (e.g., the poor, disabled and marginalised) are provided even extra help to resources for access to education. This means taking into account relative as well as physical access. Although the physical library may be technically accessible to all, poor families may find relative access difficult due to issues such as the cost and ease of transportation (Nichols, 2011) and the presence of knowledgeable adults able to help them navigate the space and use of the public library (Jocson & Thorne-Wallington, 2013; Neuman & Celano, 2012a, 2012b). As such, school libraries play a particularly important role for students from low socioeconomic backgrounds, as they are likely to have less access to books at home (Krashen, 2004; Loh, 2014, 2016b; C. Smith, Constantino, & Krashen, 1997) and to rich literacy experiences at home (Neuman & Celano, 2001, 2012a). Neuman and Celano (2012b) argue that there is a need to "unlevel" the gap and to tip resources in favour of poor students to make up for the lack of home resources. Ensuring well-maintained, richly-resourced and well-used school libraries and support staff is thus an issue of improving the access of low-income children to books and literacy-rich experiences.

Mapping library spaces

To examine the space of the school library, I employ a socio-spatial approach to map the library spaces of Ace Independent and Tembusu Secondary. Through physical, social and affective mapping of how the space of the library is occupied and used, I make visible the kinds of discourses of reading and learning that are located in the lived spaces of these libraries. Just as political, cultural, and economic forces shape school practices and school practices are connected to networks of practices outside schools (Nespor, 1997), the organisation of the physical, social and affective spaces within the school has much to say about the organisation of the school and of knowledge. Being attentive to how space affects social relationships and vice versa allows for insight into how space can be better organised to facilitate the construction of reading identities within the school.

I focus on the school library as a microcosm of interconnected practices and ideologies using a geosemiotic approach, which "combines elements of *geography*, the study of places, with *semiotics*, the study of sign systems" (Nichols, 2014, p. 175). Created by Scollon and Scollon (2003), a geosemiotic approach demands documentation of a particular space, with attention to concepts of "space/place and signification" (Nichols, 2011, p. 169). It contributes to an ecological perspective of space by examining how sociocultural and material resources have an impact on students' use and access to space. Moreover, it highlights that the arrangement of space in terms of the organisation of space and material objects placed in that space (physical), the social relations that permeate different spaces and that are shaped by space (social), and the emotion that is linked to specific places (affective) are shaped by and reflect the dominant ideologies (political) that shape and are reflected by each space. In Scollon and Scollon's (2003) *Discourses in Place*, they describe a photograph of dinner party in Hong Kong and discuss how the social interaction that takes place is closely aligned to "the social understandings of the interaction order and the structure of the physical space and the time in which it occurs" (p. 177). They compile the "semiotic aggregate" of visual signs which include the understandings of what happens in an urban restaurant, design and organisation of space and conventions guiding social interaction, relations among the individuals at the gathering to understand the multiple discourses taking place. That space bounded within the place of the restaurant is in turn permeated by the networks and flows of other discourses outside of the physical restaurant. For example, the elder celebrating his birthday is given a place of honour facing the door, following Confucian tradition, a discourse prevalent in Hong Kong society in a particular time, sedimented by years of tradition and history into a specific convention within one society. A geosemiotic approach towards the school library must therefore attend to the symbolic value of the use of space and the interactions within the space.

Practically, the exercise of documentation for the studies was achieved through physical, social and affective mapping through detailed observations of the library space over a period of two weeks. Interviews with staff and students were conducted. To understand the school culture within which each school library is situated, classroom and school observations were also made, together with examination of school artefacts such as the school website and official curriculum documents. By physical mapping, I refer to the detailed mapping of the layout and organisation of the school library, which includes attention to materials and artefacts such as books and displays. The two-dimensional physical map does not completely capture the three-dimensional lived space, but captures the resources and organisation of resources, and is a starting point to engage in an understanding of the use of space in a particular context. Mapping the social and affective spaces (through observations and interviews), on the other hand, captures the lived social life on the ground that constitutes our social interaction, affective memories and responses to physical space (Lefebvre, 1991). Our emotional responses to particular spaces drive our choice to stay in those places, and as such, there is a need to attend to what students feel (the affective) in relation to what students do (the social) within a space. The attention to the *physical, social and affective spaces of practice* in this study is, thus, an attempt to describe, break down and examine taken-for-granted practices that may reveal a misalignment between official discourses and situated everyday practices of literacies. By examining the different dimensions of space in detail, the *political dimension* of space that underlies and shapes lived space is brought to the fore, and we can begin to understand and possibly transform the dominant discourses that shape particular spaces and the social relations and literacy practices contained within these spaces of practice.

The decision to focus on the library in this analysis stemmed largely from a specific finding from the descriptive survey conducted in Tembusu Secondary which identified the school library as a problematic space, with only 40.9% of students stating that they had visited the school library. Only 21.1% stated that they visited the school library regularly (once a month or less). Although a school-wide survey was not conducted at Ace Independent, initial observations of the Ace library showed far more traffic and use than the relatively under-utilised Tembusu library. Given that the organisation of school libraries can reveal much about the kinds of practices and habits that are preferred within each milieu and context, and can even reveal tensions between the ideal and practice (Dressman & Tettegah, 2006), a physical, social and affective mapping of the two libraries provides a way to see the contrasting values accorded to the libraries in both schools and demonstrates how knowledge is perceived and enacted in the space of the school libraries. Typical measures such as book loans, self-reported surveys, although useful to some degree, may not provide sufficient detail to explain how a library is practically utilised and why it is so.

Both libraries were, on the surface, well stocked, although Ace Independent had quantitatively more books. The Tembusu library stocked 24,000 books (which worked out to about 20 books per student), whereas the Ace library stocked 100,000 books for 1,900 students (52 books per student). Qualitatively, the book collection followed a different logic. The Ace library served both the secondary and IBDP students and thus included more research resources for the

IBDP students. On the other hand, Tembusu had an SSR programme where students were allocated a wide range of texts to read; as such, part of its collection included repeated books for entire levels. The English department heads in both schools spoke of the importance of the school library and were actively involved in the book selection and renewal process. Tembusu employed a library assistant to help with the day-to-day management of the library, whereas Ace Independent employed a trained librarian and two library assistants. Subject-teachers were responsible for the management of the library and library club for students at both schools.

Both Tembusu and Ace libraries possessed the physical signs of a school library: a librarian's desk, fiction and non-fiction books in shelves, trolleys, magazines and newspapers, some multimedia resources, sofas and armchairs to lounge on and tables and chairs for students to work at. Yet, the Tembusu Media Resource Library gave an impression of being generally empty and under-utilised, whereas the Ace Independent Library seemed filled most of the time. Mapping the physical, social and affective spaces of a school library was a way to compare what schools had and how they used their resources.

Mapping physical spaces

The organisation of the physical space of the library and the materials and resources in the school libraries form the core of this analysis. The focus is on access to space, and the material and social qualities of these spaces, to render greater insight into how space is used and experienced in relation to students' reading practices and the schools' desired reading aims. The maps of the two school libraries are visual representations of how space was prioritised and organised within the two libraries.

Size and Access. The Tembusu library consisted of a single level and was positioned in an easily-accessible location on the first floor of the school. The majority of the students would have to walk by the library on their way to the classroom or from their classroom to the canteen (or cafeteria) for their recess or lunch. Although the location was easily accessible, there was little student traffic. Sometimes, the lights were dimmed to save electricity, and it was not clear if the library was open or not. The library was also often utilised in the afternoons for events such as staff meetings or workshops and to host visitors to the school, which meant that it was not always available for student use. A small classroom that could fit about 20 people was available for reservation by teachers for teaching or other activities but was seldom used.

The Ace library was also located in a relatively accessible area of the school on the third floor. The first level was about thrice the size of the Tembusu library, and there was a second lower level where most of the non-fiction titles were housed. At the lower level, there was a large teachers' resource room with teaching resources and materials, a room set aside for counselling and two other small rooms for discussions. Like the Tembusu library, the library was sometimes closed for meetings or workshops, but library closure occurred less often as there were

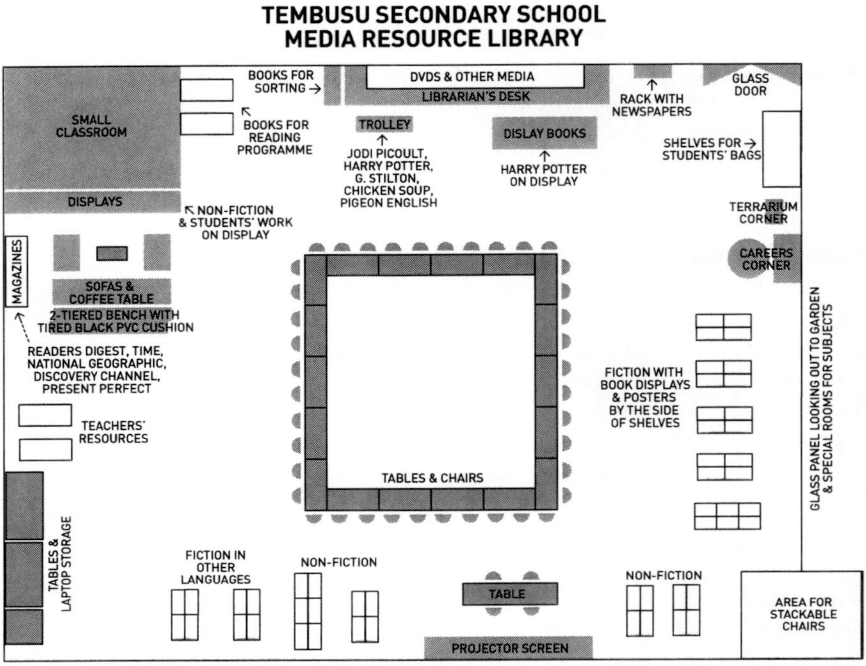

76 Levelling *the reading gap*

**TEMBUSU SECONDARY SCHOOL
MEDIA RESOURCE LIBRARY**

[Floor plan diagram with the following labels: SMALL CLASSROOM; BOOKS FOR SORTING →; DVDS & OTHER MEDIA; LIBRARIAN'S DESK; RACK WITH NEWSPAPERS; GLASS DOOR; BOOKS FOR READING PROGRAMME; TROLLEY; JODI PICOULT, HARRY POTTER, G. STILTON, CHICKEN SOUP, PIGEON ENGLISH; DISLAY BOOKS; HARRY POTTER ON DISPLAY; SHELVES FOR → STUDENTS' BAGS; DISPLAYS; ← NON-FICTION & STUDENTS' WORK ON DISPLAY; TERRARIUM CORNER; MAGAZINES; SOFAS & COFFEE TABLE; 2-TIERED BENCH WITH TIRED BLACK PVC CUSHION; READERS DIGEST, TIME, NATIONAL GEOGRAPHIC, DISCOVERY CHANNEL, PRESENT PERFECT; CAREERS CORNER; FICTION WITH BOOK DISPLAYS & POSTERS BY THE SIDE OF SHELVES; GLASS PANEL LOOKING OUT TO GARDEN & SPECIAL ROOMS FOR SUBJECTS; TEACHERS' RESOURCES; TABLES & CHAIRS; TABLES & LAPTOP STORAGE; FICTION IN OTHER LANGUAGES; NON-FICTION; TABLE; NON-FICTION; AREA FOR STACKABLE CHAIRS; PROJECTOR SCREEN]

Figure 4.1 Map of Tembusu Media Resource Library

other large rooms within the school, such as the lecture halls and large classrooms, that could be utilised for meetings. Workshops held in the library tended to be held during the school holidays, when students were less likely to be at school.

Display and Decoration: The visual semiotic (Scollon & Scollon, 2003) of place conveys the significance accorded to particular kinds of literacy events within the space. The representational space is important as it conveys a sense of the kinds of reading and learning valued at each school. At Ace Institution, the location of the panels depicting the school's history was within the library, and the walls of the library were decorated with various themed images or quotes that celebrate reading. For example, images of famous libraries, accompanied by quotes celebrating the libraries, decorated the first floor walls. In comparison, the Tembusu library was decorated with generic functional teaching posters (e.g., "Metaphors") or inspirational posters stuck onto the sides of the bookshelves. The Ace library was positioned as an archival space (of the school's history and knowledge) as well as a space for discovery about books in comparison to Tembusu's more functional focus.

There was also a notable difference in how books were selected for display. The Ace library book displays, located on shelves next to the library entrance, consisted of books curated by the librarian to privilege current informational texts and some contemporary prize-winning novels. Titles were curated to fit a wide range of interests and the IB focus on global-mindedness and research. A typical display would include non-fiction titles, biographies and fiction. In contrast, the book display at Tembusu consisted of young adult series, curated by the for-profit company managing the library rather than the librarian, and did not take into account the specific profile and programmes of specific schools. One month, I saw a display of Jodi Picoult's titles on the month of her birthday, and another month Geronimo Stilton titles were on display across different school libraries managed by the same company.

Seating, Table and Computer Access: The location of resources and organisation of space shape the social uses of the space. In Tembusu, students wishing to do online research used computers located near the school office rather than within the library. The laptops stored in the library could only be withdrawn by a teacher for classwork. At Ace, computers were located within the library near the entrance; students could be seen using the computers or seated at the nearby sofas working on their own laptops at any time of the day. The computers at the front of the library near the librarian's desk drew students into the library and added to the utility value of the library as a useful space for locating information while contributing to the symbolic value of the library as a critical space for the acquisition and application of information literacy (Kapitzke, 2003). In comparison, there was little to draw students into the Tembusu library, and students typically used laptops only under supervision of teachers, often typing their essays for submission.

In both schools, there was relatively less reading space compared to study space. In Tembusu, the only sofa set was placed in a corner of the library near the magazine section. In Ace Institution, there were three sets of three armchairs placed near the entrance of the library. Although these spaces were used for reading, they were more often than not used for students' colonised purposes of talking, discussion or doing schoolwork. Students did, however, make use of the study tables for reading. With regard to study space, the table arrangements imply particular modes of studying that are important in each context. At Ace, the tables were arranged in rows, with seating to allow independent study or small group study (See Figure 4.2). On the other hand, the tables and chairs at Tembusu were moved often, depending on the needs of the school. However, the layout in Figure 4.2, with tables arranged to make a large circle, resembling a large classroom discussion format was a regular feature. This arrangement is significant as it reflects the dominant use of the library as a large, air-conditioned classroom space for students.

The school library, while bounded, is permeated by official and unofficial discourses of what knowledge is, who accesses knowledge and how knowledge is to be used within the school and learning context. The larger space allocated to the Ace Institution library is generally reflective of the larger grounds of the independent school, but more importantly, the design and organisation of the space conveyed what was considered important for reading and learning in each school. The availability of a wide range of fiction and non-fiction at Ace was in part guided by the IBDP curriculum requirement that school libraries contribute to

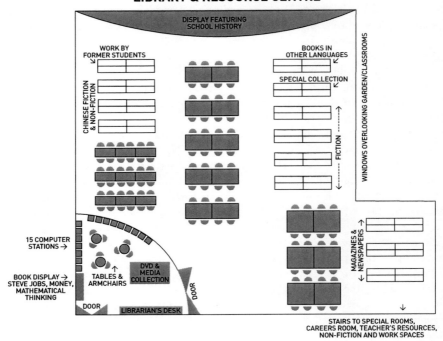

Figure 4.2 Map of Ace Institution library, top level

Figure 4.3 Layout of tables at Tembusu

Figure 4.4 Tembusu careers' corner

the task of developing internationally-minded people. The library website quoted a "Harvard University Professor Emeritus" that "what the school thinks about its library, is a measure of what it feels about education" and this was supported by the décor of the library with inspirational pictures and quotes of the importance of the library. There was a sense that the space and work of the library was integrated with the school's curriculum focus on inquiry-based learning. In contrast, the design and organisation of Tembusu's space seemed more disconnected from the work of the school. The fact that the careers' corner (see Figure 4.4) was situated at the most visible place at the entrance of the Tembusu library, and that it was nicely done up, signalled that this was an important aspect for the school. In fact, the school had a strong career guidance programme, and this emphasis was clearly conveyed through the prominent and thoughtful placement of the careers' corner with relevant brochures and books.

Mapping social spaces

The attention to the social is a deliberate attempt to observe overt behaviour that points to the spatial significance of particular organisations of space. It may confirm the how the physical layout and organisation may encourage certain social behaviour; on the other hand, one may also discover how space is used in ways contrary to official expectations. Shilling and Cousins' (1990) view of the processes of colonisation (with students using the library for unintended purposes)

Figure 4.5 Physical, social and affective comparison of Tembusu library and Ace library

	Tembusu Library	*Ace Library*
Location	First floor corner	Central block, third floor, close to staff room
Layout and organisation	To the left of the library were about 10 low shelves of fiction, which included both classics and contemporary young adult literature. At the back of the library were 12 shelves of non-fiction, and eight shelves of books in Chinese, Tamil and Malay. To the right was a display shelf with copies of magazines such as *Reader's Digest*, *Newsweek*, *National Geographic* and *Present Perfect*, a locally-produced current affairs magazine for students. A small set of sofas, seldom utilised, was beside the magazines. In the far right, there was a little room that could be used for small classes. Beside the room were two large shelves of the books allocated for the reading programme to be managed and sorted by the librarian at the end of reading cycle. Desks were organised as study desks, and the library was often used as a classroom or for staff meetings, making it difficult for students to access it. Laptops were locked, drawn out by teachers for classwork.	On the left, there were about 40 tall shelves of fiction and non-fiction. Although the library was not as well-stocked as the libraries of some other elite schools in Singapore, there were more books and a much better selection than Tembusu Secondary. They were displayed in such a way as to attract the attention of students, with constantly rotating displays, including themed displays about war or female writers. Further in, the wall on the right was lined with many magazines and newspapers including the *Straits Times*, *National Geographic*, *Runner's World* and *The Economist*. There were more specialised magazines compared to Tembusu Secondary, and unlike Tembusu Secondary, students came in to browse the magazine titles and spend time reading them. There was a display of school history at the end of the library. Space was utilised primarily as library space. Computers at the entrance of library were constantly used by students.
Display	Rotating display that changed every two months. Included books by Jodi Picoult and J. K. Rowling and books of the Geronimo Stilton series.	Monthly rotating display including fiction and non-fiction, with feedback from teachers. Included displays that were linked to special occasions or study.

	Tembusu Library	Ace Library
Staff support	One librarian to manage library; role was clerical. Library teacher-in-charge managed library, with recommendations from colleagues, and also managed library committee consisting of students.	One trained teacher-librarian and two assistants. Four teachers-in-charge managed the student committee, who worked with librarians to stock and maintain library.
Observations of social life of library	Case study students did not go to the library to borrow books; described by Kate as "absolutely deserted", and Edward noted that "no one goes in and out of the library". During recess, typically three to five students were seen going to the library to read or chat, and fewer than 10 students were observed using the library on any typical day after school. Two days out of five, the library was used as classroom or detention space after school. Students typically did written work in the library.	Case study students all went to the library to varying degrees. Sanjeev browsed the magazines, and the others tended to borrow books or use the library for work. At any time, especially during recess or after school, the library was filled with boys reading or doing their work and seemed full compared to Tembusu. Unlike at Tembusu, I saw more students checking books out of the library. Students did more research work than written work in the library.
Affective responses	Cass mentioned that the library is associated with detention and homework, and none of the case study students thought the library was a pleasant place to be in. Not seeing anyone go in or out indicated that the library was perceived as "not happening and hip". Students were not drawn into the library, although they might escape into the air-conditioned comfort of the library.	Students used the word "like" to describe their impressions of the library. It was a place they liked to go to: for some to read magazines, for others to read books and for others to do work or chat. Overall, mention of the library generated positive rather than negative feelings.

and regulation (by the librarian and other authority figures), and of association and disassociation (where different groups of students can choose whether to occupy the library or vacate it at various times) within the library space highlight that the sense of space is both regulated and resisted. Whereas those in authority may view the school library as a quiet study space or reading space, some students may resist this view of space, instead colonising the educational space for meeting friends and chatting under the guise of work. In this section, I discuss my observations of the happenings in the library, focusing particularly on the library as a reading space and as a study space. I juxtapose official expectations with actual use to understand what the library actually meant to the students and observe how the library was used in reality.

With regard to the use of the library as a study space, I saw many lessons being conducted in the library at Tembusu but seldom observed students borrowing books or using the library for research. The library was often used for some other purpose such as conducting a test or meeting after school, making it unavailable to students for reading or studying. In the one week when I observed the use of the library after school, the library was unavailable three out of five days: The library was closed for a staff meeting on one day, for a class test on another, and to host students from Vietnam on another afternoon. In fact, the layout of the library with desks set in a large circle or in rows, as well as the way it was actually used as extra classroom space, marked the library as additional classroom space rather than a central space for independent knowledge acquisition and learning about the acquisition of knowledge. The physical space implied that the library was not so much a social space for interacting with and about books as it was a space for enforced work. This perception of the library as a space for enforced work was reinforced by the fact that the library was the place where students were sent to for detention.

In comparison, although students were also brought to the Ace library for work, the nature of the work differed. Although students were sent to the library to complete written work at times (including the completion of late work), I observed that teachers mostly brought their teachers to the library for research-based work such as project work, where students had to come up with their own research questions for independent research. Samples of exemplary student work were kept on a back shelf in the library, and I observed the older students coming in to reference these works in preparation for their own research. Students also often had their own laptops, which they brought to the library to complete their work. The use of the library was modelled by some teachers who taught their students to use the resources in the library and online to find necessary information.

Mapping the social life of the library with a comparative lens brought up the fact that both libraries were often utilised by teachers for classroom work but that the differing nature of classroom work set the tone for the students' perception of the *utility value* of the libraries. At Tembusu, students were often brought to the library to complete written work on the laptops that were kept away unless requested by a teacher for classwork. In comparison, the perceived work of the library at Ace Institution included group work and research. The nature of classwork completed in the library affirmed for Ace students the need to independently search for information, whereas there was a more functional approach towards knowledge at Tembusu, with the focus on completion of written work.

In terms of reading spaces, there was little sofa space in both libraries for reading, and these spaces were often colonised for other purposes such as chatting, group discussion or independent work rather than reading or activities around reading (e.g., book discussions). There was one sofa set beside the magazine shelf at Tembusu, but the titles (such as *National Geographic*, *The Economist*, *Present Perfect* and education-related publication) were pristine and seldom used. At Ace, the three armchair sets at the entrance of the library were conducive to smaller groups chatting, but as in Tembusu, the space was colonised for other social purposes rather than reading. What differed was that there were a greater variety of magazines, including specialist magazines to do with topics such as photography or sports, and students tended to browse through these magazines more often, usually sitting at the nearby tables and chairs. The greater variety of magazines was a draw for Ace students who might not have subscribed to these specialist magazines. Providing books or magazines that students *want* to read is one way to draw them into the social space of the library (Atwell, 2007; Gabriel, Allington, & Billen, 2012; Worthy, Moorman, & Turner, 1999). Book displays, while seemingly static, play an important role in drawing students to read and to read different kinds of texts.

What was also absent in both library spaces was organised programmes centred on reading (e.g., book clubs or reading competitions) in contrast to primary school libraries. This could be due to the perception that secondary school students no longer require that sort of reading encouragement. However, the encouragement to continue reading and to develop habits of extensive reading may still be crucial at the transition years from primary to lower secondary (Laurenson, McDermott, Sadleir, & Meade, 2015; Merga, 2015). The absence of programmes actively promoting a social life around books and reading is striking given the emphasis on the importance of reading in both English departments.

Mapping affective spaces

The affective responses of students to a space, derived from interviews with the students, explained why the libraries were used as they were. Tembusu students, especially the low-achieving and low-SES students, were not motivated to use the library because of their perception of the library as being unattractive and lacking in social value. In my interviews with 12 students, the word "boring" recurred at least six times, among other descriptions, when asked to describe the Tembusu library.

> No one goes in and out of the library. There's nothing there. It's boring.
>
> (Edward, Tembusu Secondary, avid reader)

> You only go to the library if you have detention! I never go to the library!
>
> (Cass, Tembusu Secondary, non-reader)

> I don't really go the library. I prefer to go to the entertainment room if I have time.
>
> (Yi Han, Tembusu Secondary, non-reader)

Even Edward, an avid reader who visits the public library on a weekly basis, feels that his school library is unattractive, dead space. What was striking in the interviews was that students saw the amount of activity and the type of activity in a library as indication that it was a place worth going to. The fact that "no one goes in and out of the library" (a sentiment echoed a few times by other students) reinforced the students' perception that there was nothing attractive there. Moreover, the fact that the school library is used for detention contributes to students' negative emotional responses. Already busy with schoolwork and co-curricular activities, students who could relax found the entertainment room located at a prime location near the canteen far more attractive than the library. Kate, another student, suggested that "a complete revamp, with bean bags and all" might draw her into the library, thus pointing to the affective as a necessary component for engagement (M. W. Smith & Wilhelm, 2002). Students are drawn by the social life of a place to participate within the space.

Unlike the Tembusu students, the Ace Institution case study students *liked* their library, even though there were varying degrees of use. "Like" was a word often used to describe library.

> Sometimes, during recess, I sit at the sofa, and browse through the magazines, usually *The Runner*. I don't subscribe to that at home so it's useful that it's in school.
>
> (Sanjeev, Ace Institution, reader)

For example, Sanjeev, a school runner and prefect, did not need to go to the library to borrow fiction as his parents allow him to purchase books, but he still saw the library as a space to relax and read *The Runner*, a magazine he does not subscribe to at home. Joel, a school librarian, talked about "hanging out" in the library after school and borrowing recommended books for his leisure reading. In fact, he had picked up Ayn Rand's *The Fountainhead*, a difficult philosophical read and one of his favourite books during library duty. Others such as Mark and Robert reported using the library less for reading, as they had easy access to more books via bookstores or the public library, but talked about using it after school occasionally to do their work or for research. It was a place they independently and willingly stepped into when required or desired. The positive affective responses of Ace Institution students generally meant that they saw value in using the library and were motivated to use it. More importantly, it was a place they used voluntarily and independently, without teacher supervision or imposition. This familiarity with the library was likely supported by their early home practices (see Chapter 2).

The affective was recognised as an important element in the design and management of the Ace library, unlike Tembusu's more functional library. Although there were attempts to cultivate a reading culture at Tembusu, the attempts were aimed at remediating the reader and failed to acknowledge that students may not buy into dominant strategies to improve themselves because of their own reader histories and non-existent or negative relationships with books, reading and schooling (Hicks, 2002). The different reader histories and relationships with books, reading and schooling are particularly striking when comparing the practices and responses of the high-achieving boys from Ace and the low-achieving boys from Tembusu. For the high-achieving boys who fall into the category of "can read, do read freely" (Moss, 2007), they had acquired identities as readers and willingly engaged in texts, without the need for prompting. They were independent, self-sufficient readers who could flexibly access different kinds of texts for different purposes (Loh, 2013b).

On the other hand, for the low-achieving boys who "can't yet, don't read" (Moss, 2007), more effort was required to engage them in books and reading that would contribute to their academic learning. The research on reading engagement points to the importance of motivation in encouraging student reading (Gambrell, 2013; Guthrie, Klauda, & Ho, 2013; Guthrie & Wigfield, 2000; Ivey & Broaddus, 2001; Moje, Overby, Tysvaer, & Morris, 2008) and how the school library can certainly be central in promoting a vibrant reading culture (Adkins & Brendler, 2015; Krashen, 2004; McKechnie & Rothbauer, 2006). Yet, if students are not emotionally connected or drawn into the library, they are not able to maximise the library's resources for reading and learning.

School libraries, reading and equitable access

Although these two schools may not be representative of all schools in Singapore, the comparisons are "telling cases" (Mitchell, 1983) that provide insight into what differential resources indicate about the nature of learning in each context and how reading and learning are differently associated in the space of each school library. Clearly, in this case, Ace Institution is more richly resourced, whether in terms of the library space, the kinds of books available or the staffing that contributes to making the library space work. Whether in Singapore (Koh & Kenway, 2012) or elsewhere in the world (Bourdieu, 1989; Cookson & Persell, 1985; Kenway & Fahey, 2014; Khan, 2012), elite schools generally have more space and resources. More importantly though, this comparison of the school libraries highlights that beyond the availability of physical resources, the design and organisation of these resources to encourage particular kinds of reading and learning dispositions contribute to what students learn and how students learn. In this comparison of two school libraries, the uneven structuring of space, although unintentional, may lead to a situation where elite students with greater home resources to literacy get even more opportunities at school, whereas students who are from disadvantaged backgrounds, who may be already disinclined to read, may be disadvantaged further by the lack of resources within their own schools, specifically in the spaces of school libraries. The case studies reveal that the potential of secondary school libraries for supporting equitable reading and learning may possibly be under-utilised in Singapore secondary schools.

The socio-spatial mapping also reveals the nature of knowledge that is prioritised in the design and structuring of the libraries, one more inquiry based and the other more functional. The design and use of the school libraries in both schools reflected the symbolic and actual value accorded to the library as a space for the cultivation of reading habits and fostering critical information literacy. Attending to social and affective spaces of learning highlights students' actual usage and responses to the library and is an effective way for schools to evaluate the effectiveness of the space in promoting the kinds of learning desired. In the case of the school libraries studied in this chapter, the qualitative evaluation of the school libraries was insightful in explaining how both spaces were being perceived and used. The mapping revealed how school library design and organisation may not be tied to the overall purpose and pedagogical objectives of the school or may not cater to particular student profiles.

As such, the evaluation of learning environments must take into account more rigorous pedagogical perspectives (Cleveland & Fisher, 2014) and ensure that learning needs are met by the design and organisation of space. The location, design and management of school libraries send important messages about the importance of reading in schools (Dressman & Tettegah, 2006). The analysis revealed that effective reading intervention requires an ideological shift in the way many secondary school libraries are perceived in most schools in the Singapore context: from being peripheral homework and classroom spaces to being central spaces for reading and the acquisition of critical information practices. The conception of the library as an archive rather than a space for teaching students about critical information literacy (Kapitzke, 2003) or for engaging students in a love of reading (Ross, McKechnie, & Routhbauer, 2006) has perhaps meant that for most secondary schools, simply labelling a space as "library" is often deemed sufficient for attracting students to the space or for engaging them in reading. As this study shows, students need motivation to use the library and to engage with the kinds of reading practices associated with it.

Re-visioning the library as a central space for making reading fun may serve to draw low-achieving readers into the library and encourage reading. However, reconceptualisation of space requires understanding of how space and resources are utilised (Leander & Hollet, 2013). Mere renovation cannot inspire pedagogical change. Rather, re-organisation of space must take into consideration the kinds of pedagogical innovation and learning that space should engender. Moreover, this chapter has highlighted that spatial organisation is dictated by social relations and vice versa. As such, reorganisation of space also requires reconceptualisation of social relations within the space. In the case of reading, teachers may need to review their notions of reading to focus not just on reading instruction but think about how to create pleasurable experiences around reading in school through the school library and other spaces and programmes (Francois, 2013; Ivey, 2014). In Cremin, Mottram, Collins, Powerll, and Safford's (2014) *Teachers as Readers* study in the UK, they worked with teachers to encourage them to become "Reading Teachers – teachers who read and readers who teach" (p. 67). When teachers perceive their reading as important, read more, and share their reading practices with their students, they found increased pleasure in reading and were successful in building communities of readers with their students. Seeing themselves as readers and their reading as important required a fundamental change in their mind-sets about what constitutes meaningful reading in and out of school. These teachers are reconceptualising their role and the relation to students with regard to reading – rather than imposing reading, they read alongside students and act as mentor, cheerleader and guide to cultivate students' reading interest and engagement.

From class perspectives, the role of the school library is even more important when it serves disadvantaged populations. Neuman and Celano (2012b) pointed out in their study of the use of public libraries that the "paradox of levelling the field is that in equalizing resources, the field is still unequal" because it is not just material resources but intangible resources that contribute to middle-class children's advantage when it comes to reading development.

> We clearly see that there is a more critical factor: class- and culture-based parenting practices . . . the effects of these differing strategies – which are not only a matter of resources but also of beliefs and habits – are to reinforce class divisions.
>
> (p. 18)

Neuman and Celano highlighted the importance of mentors and programmes to engage students in learning to read and learning, particularly those who come from homes that do not support school-based literacies and ways of learning. The presence of teacher-librarians, who can actively work with non-readers or disadvantaged students to cultivate the love and the skill of reading that lead to meaningful knowledge acquisition, can go a long way towards closing the gap between students from different socioeconomic backgrounds. However, given that this is not the norm in Singapore secondary schools, policy level changes are required to ensure the requisite support for these students.

The attention to detail through the mapping of the social, affective, material and political spaces of practice in this study provides a way of seeing, a detailed reading that results in discernment of possible spaces for transformation. Adopting a comparative socio-spatial analysis with attention to practice provides a framework for schools to locate specific areas for intervention. Whereas this particular close analysis of two schools in the Singapore context reveals that school libraries can be hidden spaces of inequity in Singapore schools, applying the framework of spaces of practice to other contexts may reveal other inequities for action and transformation. Rather than viewing students as the problem, or even teachers as the solution, bringing space into the equation provides another angle from which to understand how education can be transformative rather than reproductive.

5 Conclusion
The space and practice of reading

> No matter what our personal inclinations, teachers especially can no longer obliterate the diverse voices, unashamed of their distinctiveness, speaking the life stories and cultural stories sometimes at odds with or contemptuous of the sacred wits of mainstream life. Nor can anyone hide any longer from the troubling fact that industrialized, technological societies have turned out to be fundamentally unequal ones when it comes to status and reward, that they parcel out unequal life chances. We realize now that success depends only occasionally on capacity or even merit. We realize how often it depends on original advantage, or contingency or luck. So how do public schools, presumably dedicated to equality in the midst of pluralism, even out the playing field? How do they provide more opportunities for personal, distinctive growth? How do we, as teachers, cautioned against thinking in terms of predictions and predeterminations, provoke all our students to learn how to learn in a world we and they know is neither equitable nor fair?
> —(Greene, 1995, p. 170)

The objective of this book has been to illustrate how practice and spatial perspectives can inform our understanding of reading and social class. Weis and Dolby (2012) argue that "education is still a critically important space where class is struggled over, engaged, produced, and lived out, as we simultaneously resituate the analysis in its global reality" (p. 2) in their edited collection, *Social Class and Education: Global Perspectives*. Indeed, I have argued throughout this book that there is a need to acknowledge the role of social class in influencing how adolescents come to see themselves as readers and engage with reading. Whether one reads, what one reads and how one identifies as a reader are influenced by one's access to books and reading experiences, influenced in part by one's class position. Adolescents learn to relate to books and reading in particular ways, implicated by networks of home-school connections, school-nation connections and school-space connections.

Practice and spatial perspectives make visible the invisible structures of class through attention to the network of resources which support the development of a reading identity aligned to the kinds of content, skills and dispositions that are encouraged in particular school curricula and to the spaces where reading is encouraged or discouraged within the school environment. Rather than seeing the student-as-problem, a social class lens that adopts a structure-as-problem perspective relocates the problem and provides insight into how home background, together with institutional and official policy structures, may reinforce class divisions by limiting distribution or access to resources. Recognising the inscription of social class on every practice of reading liberates educators to reimagine alternative ways of envisioning and enacting reading curriculum and instruction in local contexts. In contrast to reductionist approaches promising quick fixes or short-term success on high-stakes examinations (Alsup, 2015; Soler & Openshaw, 2006), tempting in this standards-driven age, taking a spatial and practice approach acknowledges the importance of situating understandings of reading in social and local contexts. Best practices of reading instruction and programmes, while commendable, may unknowingly reinforce deficit views or be limited in their application when there is insufficient understanding of the school and student context in which it is applied. Too often, best practices also place undue pressure on the teacher or the school as the sole change maker without recognition that systematic changes may be more effective and complement teachers' work. By attending to practice and spatial perspectives, I have sought to turn attention away from the idea of best practices towards structural and systematic issues (Bartolome, 1994; Greenleaf, Jiménez, & Roller, 2002; Hicks, 2002; Kramer-Dahl & Kwek, 2011) that educators need to engage with to better understand how to approach the teaching of reading in specific educational contexts.

Attending to practice through attention to habitus – the structuring structures (Bourdieu, 1977) of home, school and nation – is a way of mapping the misrecognized ideologies that shape daily practices of reading and learning to read. Within the Singapore context, recognising the power geometries implicated in the discourse of meritocracy and efficiency as it is played in national and individual's understandings of what it means to read and to learn to read is the first step towards identifying the unequal resources that students from different social classes bring to school. The assumed equality of meritocracy is problematic when individuals in the competition begin from different starting points in terms of home resources. Contrasting home resources of students from different social backgrounds illustrates the plentiful or lack of material and social resources for reading and explains how some students are more likely to develop a positive reading identity compared to other students.

Practice perspectives highlight that learning to read and becoming a reader is an issue of identity construction, the result of the interplay between structure and agency in everyday practices. Holland, Lachicotte, Skinner, and Cain (1998) elaborate on their concept of "improvisations" in identity making, where structure and agency both work to create new thoughts, speech and action.

> Improvisations are the sort of impromptu action that occur when our past, brought to the present as *habitus*, meets with a particular combination of circumstances and conditions for which we have no set response. Such improvisations are the openings by which change comes about from generation

to generation. They constitute the environment or landscape in which the experience of the next generation "sediments", falls out, into expectation and disposition.

(p. 18)

The promise of habitus is that it can change from generation to generation when circumstances and conditions are reworked to generate new expectations and dispositions. The invisible network of resources that students have access to may seem deterministic if used only to highlight the differential resources of students from different socioeconomic backgrounds. Class matters in that the propensity to read is developed in part through access to resources that allow for students' intensive immersion in reading. However, what the invisible network of resources also does is to make visible the oft-unrecognized resources contributing to the development of a reading identity and, as such, reveals areas where educators can work to provide opportunities in schools for students outside of the home to develop a positive relationship with reading. For example, highlighting the important role of school libraries in encouraging reading alerts schools to the importance of positioning the school library as a central space for promoting reading. Understanding that students are encouraged by other forms of media to read and vice versa means that using popular culture and other forms of media can be successfully utilised to encourage reading. Essentially, focusing on the various ways the school can make up for the lack of home resources redirects educators away from the deficit mind-set (Valencia, 2010) to engage with other structural factors that can help encourage reading in classrooms and schools.

The focus on identity in practice also highlights that reading is not *just* a disembodied skill but is tied to students' ways of valuing-thinking-talking-doing (J. P. Gee, 1996; Heath, 1986; Hicks, 2002). Whether adolescents see themselves as readers or not depends in part on whether they identify as readers or not and the kinds of readers they identify as. The adolescent boys in Smith and Wilhelm's (2002) study of adolescent boys' literacy practices choose to engage in activities that they identify with and find pleasure in. When engaged in activities they are interested in, they exhibit Csikszentmihalyi's (1996) concept of flow, a state where they are so involved in the activity that nothing else matters. In the same way, children choose to join the "literacy club" when they identify with the people and the activities in the club. F. Smith (1988) explained that children do things when they identify with the people and the activities in the club. By virtue of middle-class children's home "schooling" in reading, where they acquire a certain competence, preference and attitude towards reading, students from these homes tend to buy into reading more easily. Students from homes where reading is not the norm are more likely to exclude themselves unless there are persuasive reasons (such as a strong culture of reading in school, peers who read, role models such as teachers and other adults) for them to want to join the club.

Examining how adolescent students become readers by focusing on how they learn to identify as readers through the lenses of social class allows educators to explore issues of access from a different angle: Are students unable to identify as readers as a result of their past histories with books and readings, both at home and at school? What kinds of books can be provided for students at different levels of reading competency and engagement? What can schools do to create spaces for students to learn to identify as readers? It is no easy task to encourage students who do not have a history and family background of engaging with school-approved ways of reading to engage in reading. Qualitative studies of early childhood and primary school literacy reveal the tensions between home and school practices (Hicks, 2002; Solsken, 1993). The research discussed in this book does not track the tensions between home and school practices, but it does make clear the differential access to resources that supports the development of a reading identity. The evidence from other research of adolescent literacy also does suggest that tensions that exist between home and school environments can impede students' learning or be successfully utilised to engage students in learning, for example, through culturally relevant pedagogies (e.g., Lee, 2001; Moll, Amanti, Neff, & Gonzalez, 1992).

I have also argued in this book that taking a critical spatial approach alongside the attention to practice highlights how schools provide students with access to resources for developing a reading identity within actual school contexts. The issue of distribution is not just a matter of physical resources but also of manpower resources and students' affective relation to reading and spaces of reading within school (Loh, 2016c). Policy can be unequal in expecting differing standards from different kinds of students, for example, in the standards of critical thinking and English competency that is expected of students. Another less obvious way that policy can be unequal is when resources are not fairly allocated to areas of need, an issue that I will elaborate on later in this chapter. By focusing on spatial distribution and social relations within the bounded context of a specific school, it is possible to relook at old practices with new lenses to see how existing practices may not encourage the kinds of effective and equitable practices desired. The spatial turn reaffirms the need to rethink structural and systematic challenges, to redirect the gaze from the student and the teacher to the systems (nationwide and school-wide) that reinforce inequity or encourage equitable learning.

In Massey's (2005) *For Space*, she expresses her concern with the way we imagine space – both at local and global level – and suggest that the way space is imagined can either constraint or open up new possibilities, new ways of thinking and new ways of doing.

> *Firstly*, that we recognize space as the product of interrelations, as constituted through interactions, from the immensity of the global to the intimately tiny. *Second*, that we understand space as the sphere of the possibility of the existence of multiplicity in the sense of contemporaneous plurality; as the sphere in which distinct trajectories coexist; as the sphere therefore of coexisting heterogeneity. *Third*, that we recognize space as always under construction. Precisely because space on this reading is a product of relations-between, relations that are necessarily embedded material practices which have to be carried out, it is always in the process of being made. It is never finished; never closed.
>
> (p. 9)

Massey argues for a conception of space as relational multiple and open. In so doing, she refuses to see space as constructed by a single master narrative, even though space is all too often perceived as hegemonic and static. Using postcolonial retellings of modernity, Massey explains how the postcolonial re-narrativisation that decentres Europe makes possible a different way of understanding and of telling.

> Once understood as more than the history of Europe's own adventures, it is possible to appreciate how the previous way of telling the story (with Europe at its centre) was powered by the way in which the process was experienced *within* Europe; told from the point of view of Europe as the protagonist. *Spatialising that story enables an understanding of its positionality, its geographical embeddedness; an understanding of the spatiality of the production of knowledge itself.*
>
> (p. 63, italics mine)

Our understandings of the world are thus produced through the stories, myths and legends inscribed and re-inscribed through the media, through school textbooks and teaching methods and through our interactions with others. These master narratives intersect with personal and institutional habitus to inscribe particular ways of thinking, talking and doing. By spatialising our understanding of *habitus*, we begin to see *habitus* as fluid and porous, multiple and relational, dominated and negotiated by the individual within various competing discourses that demand particular ways of looking at the world and influence the way we think, talk and act. Seeing habitus as "stories so far", a phrase Massey continually returns to, reminds us that *habitus* is not predetermined and fixed but that different ways of visioning may provide a different way of seeing or telling to provoke a different way of acting. Thinking about *habitus* as a space of practice invites us to question the different trajectories that may invade or dominate that space differently and question the value and valuing of dominant discourses.

Constantly asking "what if" (Massey, 2005) is one way to rethink current perceptions and ways of teaching and to unearth spaces of inequity, both physical and relative. Some possible questions for rethinking reading policy, curriculum and instruction might include the following:

- What if educators focused on reading engagement rather than reading instruction?
- What if we redefined what would count as successful reading?
- What if we expect all students to learn a critical reading stance, regardless of stream or ability?
- What if we rethought the way we assess reading to include students' responses to reading rather than mere comprehension?
- What if school libraries were more conducive spaces for reading?
- What if more spaces in schools were dedicated to encouraging reading?

Deliberately seeking to understand how students access reading and how schools may not be effectively encouraging the development of reading in school is in fact a hopeful exercise. Mapping the ground and re-examining it through the lenses of structure-as-problem alerts educators to policy, curriculum and pedagogical gaps in each school's reading programme. In this final chapter, I offer some implications and suggestions for rethinking reading policy, curriculum and instruction by engaging with three key "what if?" questions.

1. What if we considered the place of emotion in reading?
2. What if we considered issues of access and distribution in reading?
3. What if we considered different ways of reading?

Reimagining reading in schools

What if we considered the place of emotion in reading? The case for engaged reading

One problem with the current crisis mentality in various parts of the world with regard to reading is the tendency to turn to technicist approaches towards learning to read, with greater emphasis in primary classrooms on phonics and decoding (Alsup, 2015; Comber, 2016; Cummins, 2015; Soler & Openshaw, 2006). This back-to-basics emphasis is reflected in secondary school classrooms where reading ability is measured by students' ability to score on reading comprehension assessments. Within Singapore, the emphasis on academic achievement and certification, the importance placed on examinations and the competition encouraged by meritocracy has led to an education system driven by an "examination-type literacy" (Cheah, 1998), where teaching and learning objectives are often directed by demands of the examination paper. This examination-oriented culture works against policy and pedagogical innovations as teachers tend to focus more on test practice and examination-oriented skills (Curdt-Christiansen & Silver, 2012; Kramer-Dahl, 2007).

The tenacity of the examination-oriented mind-set affects teachers' willingness and ability to engage in innovative practices. In Building Communities of Readers (BCR), a project to encourage English literature teachers' personal engagement with reading, researchers and teacher-educators at the NIE attempted to provide professional development opportunities in two schools by encouraging the teachers to read non-prescribed school texts and to participate in reading circles. The project failed when teachers refused to engage with professional development that did not seem immediately relevant to the examination demands, and the researchers had to abandon the "teachers-as-readers" framework (Albright, Kramer-Dahl, & Kwek, 2008). The teachers' educational history and beliefs about their students and teaching caused them to think that the BCR framework was irrelevant to their professional development needs, and in the end, the researchers had to take a more skills-oriented approach to professional development to persuade teachers to buy in to the project. During the professional development sessions, the teachers often focused on curriculum coverage or tried to make links between text and strategy to what students were studying.

This research story illustrates the pedagogical instrumentality that Singapore teachers bring to their teaching and their functional views of language learning. It is hardly surprising then that students themselves adopt such views of learning. At Tembusu, the school-wide survey of the students' reading practices revealed that a large majority of students associated reading with functional purposes, suggesting a pragmatic, instrumentalist view towards reading. Clearly, the students had absorbed the official discourse of reading as an important activity for academic achievement. However, although they had internalised the school's functional discourses towards reading and were persuaded of the value of reading, they were not necessarily motivated to read despite the school's strong emphasis on reading and the SSR programme which encouraged the students to read daily. The school's programme reflected the tension between the desire to encourage reading for pleasure and the examination emphasis that prioritises outcomes and skills-based pedagogies not uncommon in Singapore secondary schools (Wolf & Bokhorst-Heng, 2008).

To bring emotion or the affective into educators' understanding of reading is not a new idea, although it is all too often ignored in practice or forgotten when the demands of high-stakes testing overwhelm curriculum space and time. Studies of adolescent reading focus on motivation (Francois, 2013, 2015; Ivey & Broaddus, 2001; M. W. Smith & Wilhelm, 2002; Wilhelm, 2016), arguing that it is students' desire to read that ultimately leads to successful implementation of reading programmes and encourages reading engagement. One feature of whether a school is a reading school is to see whether the students desire a reading identity for themselves (Calkins, 2001; Francois, 2013). In Francois's (2013) study of how one school successfully transformed itself into a reading school, she traces how the school essentially created a "literacy-focused community of practice" where "students had enough breathing room to affirm themselves as readers in a community" (p. 3). The literacy-focused community of practice was supported by the school and classroom libraries, adults such as the principal and teachers modelling reading and student participation in book clubs, free choice reading and book discussions. Key to project success was the devotion of time and space for independent reading and adults who modelled the kind of engaged reading they desired from students. Singapore teachers do not read a lot (Cox & Schaetzel, 2007; K. K. J. Loh, 2009), and it may be that more time needs to be allocated for teachers so there is space to read. Findings from OECD's (2013) Teaching and Learning International Survey (TALIS) showed that Singapore teachers work the hardest in the world at 47.6 hours but that only 17.1 hours are spent teaching. In comparison, Finnish teachers spend 20.6 hours out of 31.6 working hours teaching (Salberg, Ravitch, & Hargreaves, 2014). Reading needs to be seen as teaching, and time needs to be set aside for *just* reading and doing activities around reading.

In a detailed analysis of pleasure that adolescent students obtain from their reading, Wilhelm (2016) pointed out that adolescent readers obtain different kinds of pleasures from their reading: immersive play pleasure, intellectual pleasure, social pleasure, the pleasure of work and the pleasure of inner work.

Immersive play pleasure, which is essential to engaged reading, is the pleasure obtained from being completely immersed in a story or a book. Intellectual pleasure is the pleasure of being immersed in the inquiry such as trying to figure out what happens next in the book. This most resembles school demands of reading. For social pleasure, there are two elements: the pleasure of using books to connect with others who have read the same or similar books and pleasure of identifying with characters in the books. Seeing self or other worlds in books allows students to develop greater confidence in their social worlds. The pleasure of work is obtained when students are able to use the reading for other goals, such as understanding others and self and using the reading for their own writing. Finally, the pleasure of inner work is when the readings help the students to understand themselves more and become "the kind of people they wanted to become" (p.36). Wilhelm noted that schools all too often focus extensively on intellectual pleasure and in the process may even interfere with students' desire to read. Schools need to allow time for students to read for enjoyment.

Considering the affective requires attention to the role of the social in encouraging reading. The cultural capital acquired by middle-class children in the area of book reading is acquired through their early exposure to a social life around books, whether through interaction with family and friends or visits to libraries and bookstores. The centrality of reading to everyday life is evident in their lived worlds. In *Reading Beyond the Book*, where Fuller and Sedo (2013) examine the social practice of contemporary reading by examining various mass reading events (MREs), which include televised book clubs such as Oprah's Book Club started in 1996 and the One Book, One Community (OBOC) reading model started in Seattle, Washington, in 1998. One important observation they make is the need to reconsider the notion of the book as codex and reading as a solitary, individualised activity (Long, 1993) and instead reframe reading as a media experience where multiple readings intersect, including the concept of reading as fun. The idea of fun includes notions of "entertainment and spectacle, social connection, intimacy, and perhaps, a sense of belonging" (p. 249). To draw students from non-reading homes into the reading experience, there is a need to encourage a sense of belonging and to encourage students to want to belong to this community of readers. Across case studies of effective reading programmes, features such as time for independent reading, free choice of books, adult modelling, and space for discussion about books are all factors contributing to the programme's success, success measured by students' increased interest in reading and perception of the school culture as one supporting reading (Cremin, Mottram, Collins, Powerll, & Safford, 2014; Francois, 2013, 2015; Ivey & Broaddus, 2001). There is a social life around books in reading schools.

However, it is also vital to evaluate the reading practices in school to determine if they cater only to particular kinds of readers. Fuller and Sedo (2013) caution from their studies of MREs that it is possible for most MREs to effect little social change as the format and style may attract the same kinds of readers from middle-class backgrounds. Alternatively, they also demonstrate that it is possible for community-based MRE models to shift what counts as reading and who qualifies as a reader through grassroots movements, thus expanding the readership profile. In the same way, schools need to closely examine their reading programmes to evaluate if they reach out only to particular student profiles. When designing programmes to appeal to adolescent readers, it is important to consider whether they reach out to avid, reluctant or struggling readers. For example, understanding that the less competent readers preferred series books in the Tembusu study meant that it was important for the school library to stock these series books. Also, strategies such as read alouds might be useful for drawing struggling readers into reading. The point is that it is important to consider how students feel about reading and to draw on the affective in encouraging student reading.

What if we considered issues of access and distribution in reading? The case for equitable reading

As discussed in Chapter 4, fair and equitable access and distribution of reading sources are not limited to physical resources but should include relative access to books and reading experiences. It has been said that Singapore is a middle-class society, with some 80% of Singaporeans owing the residential properties they live in since the late 1980s (E. S. Tan, 2015). However, a conversative estimate using the Average Household Expenditure on Basic Needs Measure (AHEBN) applied to the 2011 Department of Statistics Key Household Characteristics and Household Income Trends, 2011 reports that 11,000 to 14,000 Singaporean households have difficulty meeting basic needs (Lien Centre for Social Innovation, 2015). In a BBC article featuring Nurhaida Binte Jantan, a 29-year-old single mother with six children from five to 13 years old, who lives in a one-room flat and survives on S$600 a month and some money from a boyfriend (Leyl, 2014), the plight of the invisible poor in Singapore is highlighted. Nurhaida shared that she is unable to work as she has to look after the children and that "no one can afford to get sick in this house because our finances are too tight". In such a household, money to purchase books would be a luxury. It is clear from such examples that policies beyond educational policies need to support the creation of educational opportunities (Anyon, 2005), but the question here is how the school system can mediate the consequences of poverty.

A meritocratic system that favours competition without attention to the uneven starting points of such individuals leaves disadvantaged children behind. If reading is a significant contributor to helping children from disadvantaged homes to greater independent learning (Cummins, 2015; OECD, 2010b; Sullivan & Brown, 2013) for greater long-term mobility, more must be done to ensure equitable access to such students. At the same time, contextualising the concept of social justice and equitable access in the Singapore context requires recognising the multidimensional and relational nature of justice in specific contexts of enactment (Gewirtz, 2006). With regard to reading in the Singapore context, although the NLB has played a key role in promoting reading, it may be that the disadvantaged need even more help to access the kinds of physical resources and identities connected to reading. In terms of public access to reading, NLB has ensured that there are well-stocked public libraries conveniently located on different parts of the island. In total, there are 26 libraries located in Singapore – a large number for the island-state's total land area of approximately 720 km². Public outreach programmes such as READ@school, where NLB works actively with schools to promote reading in schools, and the kidsREAD programme, which reaches out to low-income families, are laudable but may have limited reach. For example, in a household like Nurhaida's, even the cost of transportation to access public libraries would be a luxury when there are so many basic needs to be met.

Reimagining how reading can be made more accessible to disadvantaged students means thinking out of the box, which in the Singapore context tends to mean thinking beyond better methods for reading instruction and strategies. Re-thinking the space of the school library (often referred to as school media resource libraries (SMRLs) as a central space to encourage the development of reading habits and identities is one way to rethink how access to reading is equitably distributed for easy access. As school libraries are located in schools, they can be more effectively utilised to encourage reading and learning and make up for some students' lack of access to books and rich reading experiences at home. Although early childhood and primary schooling are the best places to begin such work, secondary schools need to continue the work or address the gap where students may have slipped through the cracks in their earlier schooling. Reimagining students' access to reading opportunities in this case requires rethinking the kinds of resources (beyond classrooms and teachers) that can make up for the lack of books at home and home reading environments (Smith & Krashen, 1997).

Resources should not just include physical resources such as a space or books, which are typically provided in Singapore secondary school libraries. Keeping in mind the importance of identification with reading, and the affective value required to motivate student reading, it is worthwhile to consider how to design and organise library space and programmes to encourage student reading. It is through experiences that individuals learn to attach meaning to specific places (Tuan, 1977), and considering kinds of experiences and programmes that can encourage student belonging and engagement is one way to evaluate the suitability of library spaces and reading programmes associated with it. Designing spaces to encourage reading and learning may include the consideration of features such as furniture, soundproofing, colour and light that can improve pedagogical function (Sullivan, 2015).

Another way to rethink access would be the inclusion of teacher-librarians or more trained staff for school libraries to provide programmes, guidance and mentorship to help students less accustomed to reading and using libraries to familiarise themselves with the space and the learning that typically should take place in a library (Neuman & Celano, 2012b). Trained personnel can also provide more holistic direction for the role of the school library in encouraging reading and learning. Unlike schools in the United States, Canada or Australia, there is no mandate for Singapore secondary schools to employ teacher-librarians to manage the library. Typically, the job of managing the library is delegated to a subject-teacher, and clerical help in the form of a library assistant is employed to manage the day-to-day administrative matters. Often, the amount of attention and resources allocated to the school library depends on the support of the school principal and the culture of each school. Despite various recommendations in the early 2000s to improve Singapore school libraries through measures such as improving the status and qualifications required of the library supervisor, devoting more time and courses to teacher and librarian training, and providing opportunities for teachers and librarians to collaborate with teachers, community and curriculum planners (M. M. Gee, 1999; Majid, Chaudhry, Foo, & Logan, 2002; Mokhtar, 2003; Mokhtar & Majid, 2005; C. N. Tan, 2003; Tsai, 2001), little has been achieved in terms of explicit government policy with regard to how school libraries should be managed and teachers or librarians trained. Clearer direction from the MOE regarding opening hours, the requirement for trained library staff, and professional development of library coordinators, teachers and library assistants are some ways policy can contribute to greater awareness of the centrality of the library. Providing sufficient funding for reorganisation of space, training and purchase of books and other equipment is another important aspect that policy can contribute to.

At the school level, principals and teachers can evaluate current library usage to determine how central the school library is to the reading and learning life of the school. The importance of school administration and school-wide support cannot be understated (Everhart, 2014; Francois, 2013). Library coordinators need to make use of evidence-based research (Ross, 2006) to track library usage and effectiveness and to continually monitor how improvements are contributing to the building of a reading culture in their own schools. In terms of re-organisation of library space, library coordinators can decide on the kinds of learning objectives suitable for the specific school and student profile, in light of the school's learning objectives, and work towards cultivating those objectives over a period of time. Understanding that students need to be motivated, to be *drawn* into the library means that attention should paid to whether the space and programmes do in fact attract students. Closer attention can be paid to what students do in the library to refine the space and programmes (Loh, 2015). Because manpower is a key element for school library success, there may be a need at policy level to provide more training and time for library coordinators. It may be helpful to look to Australia, the United States or other countries with teacher-librarian systems to better understand how the current library coordinator system in Singapore can be improved. Ironically, there have been cuts in systems that have historically placed importance on teacher-librarian such as the United States (Hochman, 2016; Rosales, n.d.), despite the evidence that well-trained librarians can contribute significantly to the reading culture of schools and to academic achievement (Lance, 2002; Lance & Hofshire, 2012; Lonsdale, 2003; Todd & Kuhlthau, 2005). This is in contrast to the prevailing attitude at international schools (at least in Singapore) where the school library is perceived as an important mediator of learning and where strong school library networks exist to improve practice based on current research and practice (International School Libraries Network [Singapore], 2016).

Within the Singapore context, perhaps the efficiency and reach of the NLB, a key player in providing public access to books and knowledge, has led to insufficient attention being paid to mainstream secondary school libraries. Hochman (2016), writing about the school library situation in New York, suggests that public perception that school librarians are not vital to the school system may rest in a nostalgic remembrance of the school librarian "as a pleasant person whose work is ultimately irrelevant for contemporary schools" (p. 137). In the same way, views of the school library as an archive of print for silent reading may also act to marginalise the important work of libraries as reading and knowledge hubs. Contemporary school library research points to the importance of the school library for supporting reading (Adkins & Brendler, 2015; Knapp, 2013), collaboration and research (DelGuidice, 2015), developing critical information literacy skills (Gordon, 2010; Kapitzke & Bruce, 2006; Todd & Kuhlthau, 2005) and creating opportunities for doing, for example, through the provision of Makerspaces (Kurti, Kurti, & Fleming, 2014; Loertscher, Preddy, & Derry, 2013). However, much of the research remains within the school library and information science community and is insufficiently disseminated to the educational field. Yet, it may be that the changing contexts of the 21st-century educational field require more attention to the role of school libraries as a potential equaliser in education, and more needs to be done to understand how school libraries can be central to the cultivation of 21st-century dispositions. In the knowledge economy, there are higher expectations for what counts as basic literacies (Gee, Hull, & Lankshear, 1996). Learning to read traditional and multimodal texts critically is one aspect of acquiring 21st-century learning competencies, and reading is one way of positioning oneself as a lifelong learner. Within Singapore, the space of the school library may be a potential space for levelling the reading (and learning) gap to provide more equitable opportunities for reading (Loh, 2014).

What if we considered different ways of reading? The case for critical reading

Another way to imagine equitable reading in the Singapore context might be through the reframing of what counts as reading within school contexts and who should have access to these ways of reading. Whereas curriculum ought to be differentiated for the learning needs or learning objectives of individual students (Salberg et al., 2014), I have pointed out in Chapter 3 that the "hidden curriculum" may serve as a reproductive tool to limit access to important knowledge, skills and dispositions to students of particular class (Anyon, 1980). My argument in this chapter is that critical and imaginative ways of reading both the world and the word (Freire & Macedo, 1987) should be made available to all students through an emphasis on critical literacy. The problem with the current standards obsession results in schools trying to meet assessment standards which focus on reading comprehension tests that provide some degree of measurability and comparability across schools. This preoccupation with meeting the standards and obtaining the grades may actually impede rather than encourage reading instruction, particularly when assessment tends to be skills-oriented and limited in scope.

I have shown in the book that learning to read is not just about skills (phonics, decoding and comprehension strategies) but is also about understanding the world in which information is situated. Students acquire "information capital" (Neuman & Celano, 2012) about language, about the world and about reading that allow them to gain more knowledge about reading, language and the world (Cunningham & Stanovich, 1998; Stanovich, 1986). It is a cumulative effect. Language learning, which includes learning to read, is a values-laden enterprise (J. P. Gee, 2001; New London Group, 1996), and students also learn particular ways of reading and relating to texts through their home and school interactions (Collins & Blot, 2003; Heath, 1986). As such, learning to read is also about the acquisition of particular dispositions.

The body of work from the tradition of critical literacy tradition (Comber & Simpson, 2001; Hagood, 2004a; Janks, 2001, 2011; Luke, 2000; Luke & Freebody, 1997), while varied, generally shifts away from a linear, skills-based view of literacy learning to a view of literacy learning as socially constructed and students as active agents of literacy practices. In critical literacy classrooms,

> students and teachers together work to (a) see how the worlds of texts work to construct their worlds, their cultures, and their identities in powerful, often overtly ideological ways; and (b) use texts as social tools in ways that allow for reconstruction of the same world.
>
> (Luke, 2000, p. 453)

Taking a critical literacy approach to reading means that students need to be provided with ways to analyse different kinds of texts in their contexts of use to meaningfully reconstruct these texts for social use. Writing in the English as a second language (ESL)/English as a foreign language (EFL) context, Wallace (2003) argues that all ESL/EFL students should be exposed to a wide range of texts and learn a "global-literate English", which includes a transnational and flexible relation to language. Moreover, ESL/EFL teachers should have high expectations of their students and encourage them to learn how to dialogue with texts and about texts rather than expect plain decoding. Critical comprehension requires meaningful understanding of texts in contexts, particularly in multicultural, global contexts where there is constant need to engage with difference and the other.

This critical way of relating to language is a form of "intercultural capital" (Luke, 2004) and need not be limited to elite students. Luke and Carrington (2004) share about their professional development work in Harlow, a school in Queensland where investment in remedial action, reading recovery programmes and special education support had little impact on the long-term performance profile, despite short-term gains. They point out that the lack of success could be attributed in part to the disconnection between the technical skills-based and seemingly-irrelevant curriculum that relied on traditional print and discourse formats that alienated students. Luke and Carrington argue for a "glocalised literacy", where curriculum practice prioritises engagement with "the relationship of the local to other possible worlds" (p. 63) and encourages reflexive analysis of other and local texts. More recently, Comber's (2016) uses examples from 10 years of research in Queensland in her book *Literacy, Place, and Pedagogies of Possibility* to explain how schools and teachers can craft highly engaging and effective curriculum to engage students of poverty in learning. Drawing on place-based pedagogy, critical literacies and spatial theories, the book is full of practical illustrations of how teachers create "enabling pedagogies" to encourage student learning over the years.

Learning to read critically requires students to read widely from traditional school texts (such as literary texts and newspapers) to contemporary texts (such as young adult novels) to more varied multimodal texts (such as productions, online texts and performance poetry). Reading a wide range of texts allows students to engage with multiple texts and ways of reading to expand their textual repertoire. Learning to read critically requires students to learn to become active consumers and producers able to critically evaluate the texts they encounter in school and in their everyday experiences (Comber, 2016; Kenway & Bullen, 2008). Learning to read critically involves students' active dialogue with the text and imaginative participation in the world of the text and the world at large.

In reimagining the curriculum, the place and method of assessment needs to be re-evaluated. Assessment can contribute to the reproduction of inequities. With high-stakes tests having considerable influence on what teachers teach in the classroom, student identities that lie outside test-based norms tend to be "subtracted" from the curriculum. High-stakes tests also recontextualise what counts as knowledge and serve as a "legitimate" exclusionary device (Au, 2014). Moreover, although assessors are supposed to mark scripts without reference to a students' background, language testing, particularly when it comes to the marking of essay scripts, is influenced by the cultural discourse of dominant groups. In Kramer-Dahl's analysis of the reports of the Cambridge GCE 'O' Level Literature paper, she notes how students from non-English-speaking homes may find it hard to acquire the discourse of Western argumentation in comparison to students from middle-class English-speaking homes (Kramer-Dahl, 1999). The attraction of standards-based, skills-oriented testing is the relative ease with which students can be categorised, benchmarked and sorted based on their answers (Hudson, 2012), and emphasis on high-stakes testing to produce good results often leads to ineffective teaching that punishes students from lower-class schools, at least in the U.S. context (Spolsky, 2012). In the same way, Singapore middle-class students from English-speaking homes and able to invest in enrichment or tuition classes have greater advantage when it comes to doing well on standardised school tests. Unfortunately, in an examination-oriented system like Singapore, assessment often drives teaching. Given the importance placed on examinations, would it be possible to include a reading portfolio as part of the assessment? Would it be possible for students to demonstrate wide reading and engagement without the need to write an essay or answer comprehension questions? Could such a form of assessment encourage engaged reading? How can policy-makers and educators create a curriculum "mind-altering" curriculum (Eisner, 1998) that respects students' rights to critical reading skills? What kinds of policy, curricular and pedagogical changes need to be made for "enabling pedagogies" (Comber, 2016) to encourage students from disadvantaged backgrounds towards belonging and higher standards of learning? What would a syllabus focused on reading dispositions as well as knowledge and skills look like? How is critical thinking and creativity worked out in the practice of schools? How can assessment reflect the skills or constraint the learning? What kinds of training would teachers require to develop their own criticality and encourage critical ways of viewing language and the world within their classrooms and in their own lives?

Making the invisible visible

My argument in this book has been that social class needs to be recognised as an important consideration for informing reading policy and practice. In a largely middle-class society such as Singapore, where the competitive and self-achievement ethos of meritocracy dominate individual perceptions of merit and achievement, there is a tendency to ignore the fact that that some students come to school with more resources than others. Widening income gaps mean that middle-class parents are generally able to invest more in their children's education through strategies such as school selection, investment in tuition and enrichment classes and through the provision of physical and non-tangible resources. In terms of resource allocation, middle-class children generally have greater advantage when it comes to acquiring dispositions such as reading that are correlated to academic achievement. As such, an equitable school system needs to consider these differences to ensure that resources and strategies are provided to balance out unequal starting resources.

Within the Singapore context where teachers' beliefs and practices are influenced by years of pedagogical instrumentality to focus on skills- and examination-oriented ways of teaching (Albright & Kramer-Dahl, 2009) and where deficit views of students direct teaching and learning at schools (Kramer-Dahl & Kwek, 2011), it is important to uncover the resources that students bring to school to more effectively meet their learning needs. By assuming structure-as-problem rather than student-as-problem, educators re-adjust their lens to rethink how home resources may align or not with school demands of reading. More school stories and research stories of critical-, place- and inquiry-based learning with disadvantaged students can counteract entrenched dominant deficit discourses surrounding low-achieving students from disadvantaged backgrounds. However, extolling best practices alone is insufficient, particularly for teachers struggling to negotiate the tensions of having to meet the demands of the examination-oriented system while trying to design culturally-relevant lessons (Loh & Liew, 2016). Understanding structural and systematic inequities and working to reduce them can relieve the burden of teachers and support their work in classrooms. Making visible what is typically unrecognised thus provides a way for educators to uncover new ways of rethinking policy, curriculum and practice.

I have also argued in this book for localised understandings of how reading is understood and practiced in each context for schools to effectively develop contextualised strategies relevant to its student profile. Practice and spatial analysis can reveal the dominant discourses that shape nation and school and highlight how certain practices may obscure or perpetuate inequities. On the other hand, it also reveals areas where schools and educators can work to mediate possible inequities by providing students with the resources necessary to provide opportunities for learning to read and for developing reading identities crucial to engaged reading. It is only in reimagining the space and practice of education that alternative futures for equitable reading can be made possible.

Appendix

Data collection and analysis

For the Ace Institution study, observations of different classes and interviews with deans, teachers, current students at different grade levels, and alumni gave me a sense of the school culture. Analysis of official documents such as the school website, curriculum documents and interviews with school administration, teachers and students were also part of the data set. Case studies of six boys were conducted over the course of one year. I observed these boys over 49 classroom observations, interviewed them individually or in groups at least three times each, collected bi-monthly reading logs from them via email, and compiled field notes on a weekly basis. I also visited the library over a period of two weeks to map out the uses of the library.

The case study of Tembusu Secondary consisted of a school-wide descriptive survey of the reading practices of students, with attention to how students perceive themselves as readers and of their home and school resources for reading. A total of 1,118 students answered the survey, consisting of both closed and open-ended questions, during class-allocated time. In the second part of the study, a reading map of the school was constructed in line with the ecological approach towards reading. I observed spaces reading within the school, paying particular attention to the library as a central space for reading. Finally, I also conducted close case analyses of 12 students from two different classes and followed them over a period of three months to trace their reading habits and practices. I observed each class three times, interviewed each student individually or in focus groups twice, collected monthly updates from students via Whatsapp, a cross-platform messaging app and compiled field notes on a weekly basis.

The case study data was analysed using a constant comparison method (Charmaz, 2006) to generate key themes and insights. Both studies were analysed independently but also recursively as new insights from the second study prompted return to the data from the first study. During the first stage of data analysis, key themes were identified, and points of similarities and differences were noted between the two schools. In the second stage of the data analysis, I returned to the data to extend on and refine main themes raised in the first stage of analysis. Finally, a comparison of the physical map and social and affective map of the space of the school library followed and provided the basis for re-examining the key themes and insights raised.

References

Adkins, D., & Brendler, B. M. (2015). Libraries and reading motivation: A review of the Programme for International Student Assessment reading results. *International Federation of Library Associations and Institutions, 41*(2), 129–139.

Agnew, J. (1987). *Place and politics.* Boston, MA: Allen and Unwin.

Ahearn, L. M. (2001). Language and agency. *Annual Review of Anthropology, 30,* 109–137.

Albright, J., & Kramer-Dahl, A. (2009). The legacy of instrumentality in policy and pedagogy in the teaching of English: The case of Singapore. *Research Papers in Education, 24*(2), 201–222.

Albright, J., Kramer-Dahl, A., & Kwek, D. (2008). *Struggling against pedagogical instrumentality: Attempting to awaken the literary imagination in Singapore's Secondary English classroom.* Paper presented at the American Educational Research Association Annual Meeting, New York.

Alsup, J. (2015). *A case for teaching literature in the secondary school: Why reading matters in an age of scientific objectivity and standardization.* New York: Routledge.

Anderson, B. (1991). *Imagined communities: Reflections on the origins and spread of nationalism.* London and New York: Verso.

Anderson, R. C. (1994). Role of the reader's schema in comprehension, learning, and memory. In R. B. Ruddell, M. R. Ruddell & H. Singer (Eds.), *Theoretical models and processes of learning* (pp. 469–482). Newark, DE: International Reading Association.

Ang, I. (1982). *Watching Dallas: Soap opera and the melodramatic imagination* (D. Couling, Trans.). London and New York: Routledge.

Anyon, J. (1980). Social class and the hidden curriculum of work. *Journal of Education, 162*(1), 67–91.

Anyon, J. (2005). What "counts" as educational policy: Notes toward a new paradigm. *Harvard Educational Review, 75*(1), 65–88.

Appadurai, A. (1996). *Modernity at large: Cultural dimensions of globalization.* Minneapolis, MN: University of Minnesota Press.

Appiah, K. A. (2006). *Cosmopolitanism: Ethics in a world of strangers.* New York: W. W. Norton.

Apple, M. W. (1990). *Ideology and curriculum* (2nd ed.). London and New York: Routledge.

Apple, M. W. (1992). The text and cultural politics. *Educational Researcher, 21*(7), 4–12.

Apple, M. W. (2010). *Global crises, social justice, and education.* New York: Routledge.

Applebee, A. N. (1974). *Tradition and reform in the teaching of English: A history*. Urbana, IL: National Council of Teachers of English.
Atwell, N. (2007). *The reading zone: How to help kids become skilled, passionate, habitual, critical readers*. New York: Scholastic.
Au, W. (2014). Devising inequality: A Bernsteinian analysis of high-stakes testing and social reproduction in education. In D. Reay & C. Vincent (Eds.), *Theorizing social class and education* (pp. 77–90). New York: Routledge.
Ball, S. J. (2003). *Class strategies and the education market: The middle classes and social advantage*. New York: RoutledgeFalmer.
Barratt, L. (2010). Effective school libraries: Evidence of impact on student achievement. *The School Librarian, 58*(3), 136–139.
Barthes, R. (1974). *S/Z* (R. Miller, Trans.). New York: Hill & Wang.
Bartlett, L., & Holland, D. (2002). Theorizing the space of literary practices. *Ways of Knowing, 2*(1), 10–22.
Bartolome, L. I. (1994). Beyond the methods fetish: Toward a humanizing pedagogy. *Harvard Educational Review, 64*(2), 173–194.
Barton, D., & Hamilton, M. (2000). Literacy practices. In D. Barton, M. Hamilton & R. Ivanič (Eds.), *Situated literacies: Reading and writing in context* (pp. 7–15). London and New York: Routledge.
Bauman, Z. (1998). *Globalization: The human consequence*. New York: Columbia University Press.
Bauman, Z. (2000). *Liquid modernity*. Oxford, UK: Polity.
Beck, U. (1992). *Risk society: Towards a new modernity*. Thousand Oaks, CA: Sage.
Berliner, D. (2009). *Poverty and potential: Out-of-school factors and school success*. Boulder, CO and Tempe, AZ: Education and the Public Interest Center and Education Policy Research Unit.
Bhaskaran, M., Ho, S. C., Low, D., Tan, K. S., Vadaketh, S., & Yeoh, L. K. (2012). *Inequality and the need for a new social compact*. Paper presented at the Singapore Perspectives 2012, Singapore.
Black, R. W. (2009). Online fan fiction, global identities, and imagination. *Research in the Teaching of English, 43*(4), 397–425.
Bourdieu, P. (1977). *Outline of a theory of practice* (R. Nice, Trans.). Cambridge: Cambridge University Press.
Bourdieu, P. (1984). *Distinction: A social critique of the judgement of taste* (R. Nice, Trans.). Boston, MA: Harvard University Press.
Bourdieu, P. (1986). The forms of capital. In J. G. Richardson (Ed.), *Handbook of educational theory and research for the sociology of education* (pp. 241–258). Winsted, CT: Greenwood.
Bourdieu, P. (1989). *The state nobility* (L. C. Clough, Trans.). Stanford, CA: Stanford University Press.
Bourdieu, P., & Wacquant, L. J. D. (1992). *An invitation to reflexive sociology*. Chicago, IL: University of Chicago Press.
Boyarin, J. (1992). *Ethnographies of reading*. Berkeley, CA: University of California Press.
Brandt, D. (2001). *Literacy in American Lives*. Cambridge, UK: Cambridge University Press.
Brooks, C. (1947). *The well wrought urn: Studies in the structure of poetry*. New York: Harvest.
Brown, P. (1990). The third wave: Education and the ideology of parentocracy. *British Journal of Sociology of Education, 11*(1), 65–85.

Brown, P., Lauder, H., & Ashton, D. (2011). *The global auction: The broken promises of education, jobs and incomes*. Oxford, UK: Oxford University Press.

Buckingham, J., Beaman, R., & Wheldall, K. (2014). Why poor children are more likely to become poor readers: The early years. *Educational Review, 66*(4), 428–446.

Calkins, L. M. (2001). *The art of teaching reading*. New York: Longman.

Charmaz, K. (2006). *Constructing grounded theory: A practical guide through qualitative analysis*. London: Sage.

Cheah, B., & Robbins, B. (1998). *Cosmopolitics: Thinking and feeling beyond the nation*. Minneapolis, MN: University of Minneapolis Press.

Cheah, Y. M. (1998). The examination culture and its impact on literacy innovations: The case of Singapore. *Language and Education, 12*(3), 192–209.

Cheah, Y. M. (2002). English language teaching in Singapore. *Asia Pacific Journal of Education, 22*(2), 65–80.

Cherland, M. R. (1994). *Private practices: Girls reading fiction & constructing identity*. London: Taylor & Francis.

Chia, S. (2013, April 18). MOE focused on providing "good kindergarten education". *The Straits Times*. Retrieved from http://www.straitstimes.com/singapore/moe-focused-on-providing-good-quality-and-affordable-kindergarten-education

Chin, T., & Phillips, M. (2004). Social reproduction and child-rearing practices: Social class, children's agency, and the summer activity gap. *Sociology of Education, 77*(3), 185–210.

Chiu, M. M., & Chow, B. W. Y. (2010). Culture, motivation, and reading achievement: High school students in 41 countries. *Learning and Individual Differences, 20*, 579–592.

Choo, S. S. L. (2013). Mapping the moral, political and aesthetic objectives of English Literature education in Singapore: The period of colonisation and after. In C. E. Loh, D. Yeo & W. M. Liew (Eds.), *Teaching literature in Singapore secondary schools* (pp. 6–19). Singapore: Pearson.

Choo, S. S. L. (2014). Towards a cosmopolitan vision of English education in Singapore. *Discourse: Studies in the Cultural Politics of Education, 35*(5), 677–691.

Christian-Smith, L. K. (2001). The politics of literacies: Popular texts and young women. In P. Freebody, S. Muspratt & B. Dwyer (Eds.), *Difference, silence, and textual practice: Studies in critical literacy* (pp. 189–207). Cresskill, NJ: Hampton.

Cleveland, B. W., & Fisher, K. (2014). The evaluation of physical learning environments: A critical review of the literature. *Learning Environment Research, 17*(1), 1–28.

Collins, J., & Blot, R. K. (2003). *Literacy and literacies: Texts, power and identity*. Cambridge, UK: Cambridge University Press.

Collins, R. (1979). *The credential society: An historical sociology of education and stratification*. New York: Academic.

Comber, B. (2016). *Literacy, place, and pedagogies of possibility*. New York: Routledge.

Comber, B., Nixon, H., Ashmore, L., Loo, S., & Cook, J. (2006). Urban renewal from the inside out: Spatial and critical literacies in a low socioeconomic school community. *Mind, Culture and Activity, 13*(3), 228–246.

Comber, B., & Simpson, A. (2001). Preface. In B. Comber & A. Simpson (Eds.), *Negotiating critical literacies in classrooms* (pp. ix–xv). Mahwah, NJ: Lawrence Erlbaum.

Compton-Lily, C. (2003). *Reading families: The literate lives of urban children*. New York: Teachers College Press.

The Conference Board of Canada. (2012). *How Canada performs: Intergenerational income mobility*. Retrieved from http://www.conferenceboard.ca/hcp/details/society/intergenerational-income-mobility.aspx. Accessed on 18 October 2016.

Cookson, P. W. J., & Persell, C. H. (1985). British and American residential secondary schools: A comparative study of the reproduction of social elites. *Comparative Education Review, 29*(3), 283–298.

Corse, S. (1997). *Nationalism and literature: The politics of culture in Canada and the United States*. Cambridge: Cambridge University Press.

Cox, R., & Schaetzel, K. (2007). A preliminary study of pre-service teachers as readers in Singapore: Prolific, functional, or detached. *Language Teaching Research, 11*(3), 310–317.

Cremin, T., Mottram, M., Collins, F. M., Powerll, S., & Safford, K. (2014). *Building communities of engaged readers: Reading for pleasure*. New York: Routledge.

Cresswell, T. (2015). *Place: An introduction*. West Sussex, UK: Wiley Blackwell.

Csikszentmihalyi, M. (1996). *Creativity: Flow and the psychology of discovery and invention*. New York: HarperCollins.

Cummins, J. (2015). Literacy policy and curriculum. In J. Roswell & K. Pahl (Eds.), *The Routledge handbook of literacy studies* (pp. 231–248). New York: Routledge.

Cunningham, A. E., & Stanovich, K. E. (1998). What reading does for the mind. *American Educator, 22*(1–2), 1–8.

Curdt-Christiansen, X., & Silver, R. (2012). Educational reforms, cultural clashes and classroom practices. *Cambridge Journal of Education, 42*(2), 141–161.

Darling-Hammond, L. (2010). *The flat world and education: How America's commitment to equity will determine our future*. New York: Teachers College Press.

Darling-Hammond, L. (2012). Closing the achievement gap: A systemic view. In J. V. Clark (Ed.), *Closing the achievement gap from an international perspective* (pp. 7–20). Amsterdam, The Netherlands: Springer.

de Certeau, M. (1984). *The practice of everyday life* (S. Randall, Trans.). Berkeley, CA: University of California Press.

De Graaf, N. D., De Graaf, P. M., & Kraaykamp, G. (2000). Parental cultural capital and educational attainment in the Netherlands: A refinement of the cultural capital perspective. *Sociology of Education, 73*, 92–111.

DelGuidice, M. (2015). The role of the library in fostering research skills. *infotoday.com*, September 2015, 20–23.

Delpit, L. D. (1988). The silenced dialogue: Power and pedagogy in educating other people's children. *Harvard Educational Review, 58*, 280–298.

Demerath, P. (2009). *Producing success: The culture of personal achievement in an American High School*. Chicago and London: University of Chicago Press.

Department of Statistics Singapore. (2015a). *Education and literacy*. Singapore: Department of Statistics Singapore.

Department of Statistics Singapore. (2015b). *Population trends 2015*. Singapore: Department of Statistics Singapore.

DiMaggio, P. (1982). Cultural capital and school success: The impact of status culture participation on the grades of U.S. High School students. *American Sociological Review, 47*(2), 189–201.

DiMaggio, P., & Useem, M. (1978). Cultural democracy in a period of cultural expansion: The social composition of arts audiences in the United States. *Social Problems, 26*(2), 179–197.

DiMaggio, P., & Useem, M. (1980). The arts in education and cultural participation: The social role of aesthetic education and the arts. *Journal of Aesthetic Education, 14*(4), 55–72.

Doherty, C. (2009). The appeal of the International Baccalaureate in Australia's educational market: A curriculum of choice for mobile futures. *Discourse, 30*(1), 73–89.

Draelants, H. (2016). Changing forms of reproduction in education. In A. Koh & J. Kenway (Eds.), *Elite schools: Multiple geographies of privilege* (pp. 139–156). New York: Routledge.

Draelants, H., & Darchy-Koechlin, B. (2011). Flaunting one's academic pedigree: Self-presentation of students from elite French schools. *British Journal of Sociology of Education, 32*(1), 17–34.

Dressman, M., & Tettegah, S. (2006). Ordered by desire: School libraries in past and present times. In C. Kapitzke & B. C. Bruce (Eds.), *Libr@ries: Changing information space and practice* (pp. 37–48). Mahwah, NJ: Lawrence Erlbaum.

Druckner, P. (1969). *The age of discontinuity: Guidelines to our changing society.* London: William Heinemann.

Early Childhood Development Agency. (2013). *Government investing $30 million over the next three years on manpower efforts in early childhood sector* [Press release]. Retrieved from https://www.ecda.gov.sg/PressReleases/Pages/government-investing-$30-million-over-the-next-3-years-on-manpower-efforts-in-early-childhood-sector.aspx

Eisner, E. W. (1998). *The enlightened eye: Qualitative inquiry and the enhancement of educational practice.* Upper Saddle River, NJ: Prentice-Hall.

Elkjaer, B. (1992). Girls and information technology in Denmark: An account of a socially constructed problem. *Gender and Education, 4*(1/2), 25–40.

Epstein, D. (2014). Race-ing ladies: Lineages of privilege in an elite South African school. *Globalisation, Societies and Education, 12*(2), 244–261.

Erikson, E. H. (1968). *Identity, youth and crisis.* New York: W. W. Norton.

Everhart, N. (2014). What do stakeholders know about school library programs? Results of a focus group evaluation. *School Library Research, 17*, 1–14.

Fadzillah, I. (2005). The Amway connection: How transnational ideas of beauty and money affect northern Thai girls' perceptions of ther future options. In S. Maira & E. Soep (Eds.), *Youthscapes: The popular, the national, the global* (pp. 85–102). Philadephia, PA: University of Pennsylvania Press.

Fahey, J. (2014). Privileged girls: The place of femininity and femininity in place. *Globalisation, Societies and Education, 12*(2), 228–243.

Finders, M. J. (1997). *Just girls: Hidden literacies and life in Junior High.* New York: Teachers' College, Columbia University.

Florida, R. (2002). *The rise of the creative class.* New York: Basic Books.

Focault, M. (1995). *Discipline and punish: The birth of the prison.* New York: Vintage Books.

Forbes, J., & Lingard, B. (2013). Elite school capitals and girls' schooling: Understanding the (re)production of privilege through a habitus of "assuredness". In C. Maxwell & P. Aggleton (Eds.), *Privilege, agency and affect: Understanding the production and effects of action* (pp. 50–68). London: Palgrave MacMillan.

Francois, C. (2013). Reading in the crawl space: A study of an urban school's literacy-focused community of practice. *Teachers College Record, 115*, 1–35.

Francois, C. (2015). An urban school shapes young adolescents' motivation to read. *Voices From the Middle, 23*(1), 68–72.

Freire, P. (1970). *Pedagogy of the oppressed*. New York: Continuum.
Freire, P. (1991). The importance of the act of reading (L. Slover, Trans.). In C. Mitchell & K. Weiler (Eds.), *Rewriting literacy: Culture and the discourse of the other* (pp. 139–146). New York: Bergin & Garvey.
Freire, P., & Macedo, D. (1987). *Reading the word and the world*. Westport, CT: Bergin & Garvey.
Friedman, T. (2005). *The world is flat: A brief history of the twenty-first century*. New York: Farrar, Straus and Giroux.
Fuller, D., & Sedo, D. R. (2013). *Reading beyond the book: The social practices of contemporary literary culture*. New York: Routledge.
Gabriel, R., Allington, R., & Billen, M. (2012). Middle schoolers and magazines: What teachers can learn from students' leisure reading habits. *The Clearing House, 85*, 186–191.
Gambrell, L. B. (2013). Reading motivational engagement: Research trends and future directions. In P. J. Dunston, S. K. Fullerton, C. C. Bates, P. M. Stecker, M. W. Cole, A. H. Hall, D. Herro & K. N. Headley (Eds.), *62nd yearbook of the Literacy Research Association* (pp. 43–52). Altamonte Springs, FL: Literacy Research Association.
Gee, J. P. (1996). *Social linguistics and literacies* (2nd ed.). Oxford, UK: RoutledgeFalmer.
Gee, J. P. (2001). Reading as situated language: A sociocognitive perspective. *Journal of Adolescent and Adult Literacy, 44*(8), 714–725.
Gee, J. P. (2004). *Situated language and learning: A critique of traditional schooling*. New York: Routledge.
Gee, J. P., Hull, G., & Lankshear, C. (1996). *The new work order: Behind the language of the new capitalism*. Boulder, CO: Westview.
Gee, M. M. (1999). *The roles and training needs of library support staff in Singapore school libraries*. (Master of Science (Information Studies)), Nanyang Technological University, Singapore.
Gergen, K. J. (1994). Mind, text, and society: Self-memory in social context. In U. Neisser & R. Fivush (Eds.), *The remembering self: Construction and accuracy in self-narrative* (pp. 78–104). Cambridge: Cambridge University Press.
Gewirtz, S. (2006). Towards a contextualized analysis of social justice in education. *Educational Philosophy and Theory, 38*(1), 69–81.
Giroux, H. A. (1983). Theories of reproduction and resistance in the new sociology of education. *Harvard Educational Review, 53*(3), 257–293.
Goh, C. B., & Gopinathan, S. (2008). Education in Singapore: Development since 1965. In B. Fredriksen & J. P. Tan (Eds.), *An African exploration of the East Asian Education* (pp. 80–108). Washington, DC: The World Bank.
Goh, C. T. (1999). First-world economy, world-class home. *The Straits Times*. Retrieved from http://stars.nhb.gov.sg/stars/public/
Gopinathan, S. (1980). Language policy in education: A Singapore persective. In E. A. Afendras & E. L. Y. Kuo (Eds.), *Language and society in Singapore* (pp. 175–202). Singapore: Singapore University Press.
Gopinathan, S. (2003). Language policy changes 1979–1997: Politics and pedagogy. In S. Gopinathan, A. Pakir, W. K. Ho & V. Saravanan (Eds.), *Language, society and education in Singapore: Issues and trends* (2nd ed, pp. 19–44). Singapore: Eastern Universities Press.
Gopinathan, S. (2007). Globalisation, the Singapore developmental state and educational policy: A thesis revisited. *Globalisation, Societies and Education, 5*(1), 53–70.

Gopinathan, S., & Abu Baker, M. (2013). Globalization, the State and curriculum reform. In Z. Deng, S. Gopinathan & C. Lee (Eds.), *Globalization and the Singapore curriculum* (pp. 15–32). Dordrecht, The Netherlands: Springer.

Gordon, C. A. (2010). The culture of inquiry in school libraries. *School Libraries Worldwide, 16*(1), 73–88.

Goy, P. (2015, May 13). Singapore tops biggest global education rankings published by OECD. *The Straits Times.* Retrieved from http://www.straitstimes.com/singapore/education/singapore-tops-biggest-global-education-rankings-pubålished-by-oecd

Graddol, D. (2006). *English next.* London: British Council.

Greene, M. (1995). *Releasing the imagination: Essays on education, the arts, and social change.* San Francisco, CA: Jossey-Bass.

Greenfield, B. (2012, February 22). The world's richest countries, *Forbes.* Retrieved from http://www.forbes.com/sites/bethgreenfield/2012/02/22/the-worlds-richest-countries/

Greenleaf, C. L., Jiménez, R. T., & Roller, C. M. (2002). Conversations: Reclaiming secondary reading interventions: From limited to rich conceptions, from narrow to broad conversations. *Reading Research Quarterly, 37*(4), 484–496.

Gregory, E., & Williams, A. (2000). *City literacies: Learning to read across generations and cultures.* New York: Routledge.

Grosvenor, I., & Burke, C. (2008). *School.* London: Reaktion Books.

Guillory, J. (1993). *Cultural capital: The problem of literary canon formation.* Chicago, IL: University of Chicago Press.

Guitiérrez, K. D. (2008). Developing a sociocritical literacy in the Third Space. *Reading Research Quarterly, 43*(2), 148–164.

Gulson, K. N. (2011). *Education policy, space and the city: Markets and the (in)visibility of race.* New York: Routledge.

Guthrie, J. T., Klauda, S. L., & Ho, A. N. (2013). Modeling the relationships among reading instruciton, motivation, engagement, and achievement for adolescents. *Reading Research Quarterly, 48*(1), 9–26.

Guthrie, J. T., & Wigfield, A. (2000). Engagement and motivation in reading. In M. L. Kamil, P. B. Mosenthal, P. D. Pearson & R. Barr (Eds.), *Handbook of reading research, Volume 3* (pp. 403–421). New York: Routledge.

Hagood, M. C. (2004a). Critical literacy: For whom? *Reading Research Quarterly, 41*(3), 247–266.

Hagood, M. C. (2004b). A rhizomatic cartography of adolescents, popular culture, and constructions of self. In K. M. Leander & M. Sheehy (Eds.), *Spatializing literacy research and practice* (pp. 143–160). New York: Peter Lang.

Hall, C., & Coles, M. (1997). Children's reading choices: Questions of quality. *Use of English, 48*(2), 138–148.

Hannerz, U. (1990). Cosmopolitans and locals in world culture. *Theory, Culture & Society, 7,* 237–251.

Hargreaves, A. (2003). *Teaching in the knowledge society: Education in the age of insecurity.* New York: Teachers College Press.

Harris, T. S., & Graves, S. L. J. (2010). The influence of cultural capital transmission on reading achievement in African American fifth grade boys. *The Journal of Negro Education, 79*(4), 447–457.

Harvey, D. (2001). *Spaces of capital: Towards a critical geography.* New York: Routledge.

Harvey, D. (2009). *Social justice and the city*. Athens, GA: University of Georgia Press.
Heath, S. B. (1986). *Way with words: Language, life, and work in communities and classrooms*. Cambridge: Cambridge University Press.
Heath, S. B. (2005). What no bedtime story means. In A. Duranti (Ed.), *Linguistic anthropology: A reader* (pp. 318–342). Oxford, UK: Blackwell.
Hicks, D. (2002). *Reading lives: Working-class children and literacy learning*. New York: Teachers College Press.
Hirsch, E. D. (1987). *Cultural literacy: What every American needs to know*. Boston, MA: Houghton Mifflin.
Ho, E. (2006). Negotiating belonging and perceptions of citizenship in a transnational world: Singapore, a cosmopolis? *Social and Cultural Geography, 7*(3), 385–401.
Ho, K. W. (2011). Growth, opportunity, and inequality: Some empirics from Singapore. In H. Y. Sng & W. M. Chong (Eds.), *Singapore economy in 2010: Competitiveness, productivity and other issues* (pp. 1–15). Singapore: World Scientific.
Ho, L.-C. (2012). Sorting citizens: Differentiated citizenship education in Singapore. *Journal of Curriculum Studies, 44*(3), 403–428.
Hochman, J. (2016). School library nostalgias. *Curriculum Inquiry, 46*(2), 132–147.
Hogan, D. (2010). *Current and future pedagogies in Singapore*. Paper presented at the Redesigning Pedagogy, Singapore.
Holland, D., Lachicotte, W. J., Skinner, D., & Cain, C. (1998). *Identity and agency in cultural worlds*. Cambridge, MA: Harvard University Press.
Howard, A. (2010a). Elite visions: Privileged perceptions of self and others. *Teachers College Record, 112*(8), 1971–1992.
Howard, A. (2010b). Stepping outside class: Affluent students resisting privilege. In A. Howard & R. Gaztambide-Fernández (Eds.), *Educating elites: Class privilege and educational advantage* (pp. 79–95). Lanham, MD: Rowen & Littlefield.
Hudson, T. (2012). Standards-based testing. In G. Fulcher & F. Davidson (Eds.), *The Routledge handbook of language testing* (pp. 479–494). New York: Routledge.
IBO. (2002). *Language A1 world literature (English A1)*. Geneva, Switzerland: International Baccalaureate Organization.
International Association for the Evaluation of Educational Achievement. (2011). *Progress in International Reading Literacy Study 2011*. Retrieved June 10, 2016, from http://www.iea.nl/pirls_2011.html
International School Libraries Network (Singapore). (2016). *International School Libraries Network (Singapore): Home*. Retrieved July 8, 2016, from http://silcsing.blogspot.sg
Ivey, G. (2014). The social side of engaged reading for young adolescents. *The Reading Teacher, 68*(3), 165–171.
Ivey, G., & Broaddus, K. (2001). "Just plain reading": A survey of what makes students want to read in middle school classrooms. *Reading Research Quarterly, 36*(4), 350–377.
Ivey, G., & Johnston, P. H. (2013). Engagement with young adult literature: Outcomes and processes. *Reading Research Quarterly, 48*(3), 255–275.
Jackson, P. W. (1968). *Life in classrooms*. New York: Holt, Rinehart and Winston.
Jaeger, M. M. (2009). Equal access but unequal outcomes: Cultural capital and educational choice in a meritocratic society. *Social Forces, 87*(4), 1943–1971.

Jaeger, M. M. (2011). Does cultural capital really affect academic achievement? New evidence from combined sibling and panel data. *Sociology of Education, 84*(4), 281–298.

Janks, H. (2001). Identity and conflict in the critical literacy classroom. In B. Comber & A. Simpson (Eds.), *Negotiating critical literacies in classrooms* (pp. 137–150). Mahwah, NJ: Lawrence Erlbaum.

Janks, H. (2011). *Literacy and power*. New York: Routledge.

Jenkins, H., Kelley, W., Clinton, K., McWilliams, J., Pitts-Wiley, R., & Reilly, E. (2013). *Reading in a participatory culture: Remixing Moby-Dick in the English classroom*. New York: Teachers College Press.

Jocson, K., & Thorne-Wallington, E. (2013). Mapping literacy-rich environments: Geospatial perspectives on literacy and education. *Teachers College Record, 115*(6), 1–24.

Jones, S. A. (2015). Children reading series books: Ways into peer culture and reading development. *Changing English, 22*(3), 307–325.

Kang, T. (2008). Integrated programmes in Singapore: Choices and challenges. In J. Tan & P. T. Ng (Eds.), *Thinking schools, learning nations: Contemporary issues and challenges* (pp. 191–205). Singapore: Pearson/ Prentice Hall.

Kapitzke, C. (2003). (In)formation literacy: A positivist epistemology and a politics of (out)formation. *Educational Theory, 53*(1), 37–53.

Kapitzke, C., & Bruce, B. C. (2006). *Libr@ries: Changing information space and practice*. Mahwah, NJ: Lawrence Erlbaum.

Kenway, J., & Bullen, E. (2008). The global corporate curriculum and the young cyberflâneur as global citizen. In N. Dolby & F. Rizvi (Eds.), *Youth moves: Identities and education in global perspectives* (pp. 17–32). New York: Taylor & Francis.

Kenway, J., & Fahey, J. (2014). Staying ahead of the game: The globalising practices of elite schools. *Globalisation, Societies and Education, 12*(2), 177–195.

Kenway, J., & Koh, A. (2013). The elite school as "cognitive machine" and "social paradise": Developing transnational capitals for the national "field of power". *Journal of Sociology, 49*(2/3), 272–290.

Khan, S. R. (2012). *Privilege: The making of an adolescent elite at St. Paul's*. Princeton, NJ: Princeton University Press.

Khoo, M., & Ng, S. M. (1985). Reading instruction in lower primary classes: A second observational study. *Singapore Journal of Education, 7*(2), 55–64.

Kirsch, I., de Jong, J., Lafontaine, D., McQueen, J., Mendelovits, J., & Monseur, C. (2002). *Reading for change: Performance and engagement across countries*. Paris, France: Organisation for Economic Co-operation and Development.

Kliebard, H. M. (2004). *The struggle for the American Curriculum (1893–1958)* (3rd ed.). New York: RoutledgeFalmer.

Knapp, N. F. (2013). Cougar readers: Piloting a library-based intervention for struggling readers. *School Libraries Worldwide, 19*(1), 72–90.

Koh, A. (2010). *Tactical globalization: Learning from the Singapore experiment*. Singapore: Peter Lang.

Koh, A. (2013). A vision of schooling for the twenty-first century: Thinking schools and learning nation. In Z. Deng, S. Gopinathan & C. K.-E. Lee (Eds.), *Globalization and the Singapore curriculum: From policy to classroom* (pp. 49–66). London: Springer.

Koh, A., & Chong, T. (2014). Education in the global city: The manufacturing of education in Singapore. *Discourse: Studies in the Cultural Politics of Education, 35*(5), 625–636.

Koh, A., & Kenway, J. (2012). Cultivating national leaders in an elite school: Deploying the transnational in the national interest. *International Studies in Sociology of Education, 22*(4), 331–351.

Kramer-Dahl, A. (1999). Reproducing disadvantage: The discourse of GCE-O-Level Literature Examination Reports. In S. H. Chua & W. P. Chin (Eds.), *Localising pedagogy: Teaching literature in Singapore* (pp. 40–60). Singapore: National Institute of Education, Nanyang Technological University.

Kramer-Dahl, A. (2007). Teaching English Language in Singapore after 2001. In V. Vaish, S. Gopinathan & Y. Liu (Eds.), *Language, capital, culture* (pp. 47–71). Rotterdam, The Netherlands: Sense.

Kramer-Dahl, A., & Kwek, D. (2011). "Reading" the home and reading in school: Framing deficit constructions as learning difficulties in English classrooms. In C. Wyatt-Smith, J. Elkins & S. Gunn (Eds.), *Multiple perspectives on difficulties in learning: Literacy and numeracy* (pp. 159–178). Dordrecht, The Netherlands: Springer.

Krashen, S. D. (2004). *The power of reading: Insights from research* (2nd ed.). Portsmouth, NH: Heinemann.

Kurti, R. S., Kurti, D., & Fleming, L. (2014). The philosophy of educational makerspaces: Part 1 of making an educational makerspace. *Teacher Librarian, 41*(5), 8–11.

Lam, W. S. E. (2006a). Culture and learning in the context of globalization: Research directions. In J. Green & A. Luke (Eds.), *Review of research in education: Special issue on Rethinking learning: What counts as learning and what learning counts* (pp. 213–238). Washington, DC: American Educational Research Association.

Lam, W. S. E. (2006b). Re-envisioning language, literacy, and the immigrant subject in new mediascapes. *Pedagogies: An International Journal, 1*(3), 171–195.

Lamont, S., & Lareau, A. (1988). Cultural capital: Allusions, gaps and glissandos in recent theoretical developments. *American Sociological Association, 6*(2), 153–168.

Lance, K. C. (2002). What research tells us about the importance of school libraries. *Knowledge Quest, 31*(1), 17–22.

Lance, K. C., & Hofshire, L. (2012). *Change in school librarian staffing linked with change in CSAP reading performance, 2205–2011*. Denver, CO: Denver Colorado State Library, Library Research Service.

Lareau, A. (1989). *Home advantage: Social class and parental intervention in elementary education*. New York: The Falmer Press.

Lareau, A. (2003). *Unequal childhoods: Class, race and family life*. Berkeley, CA: University of California Press.

Lareau, A., & Horvat, E. M. (1999). Moments of social inclusion and exclusion: Race, class, and cultural capital in family-school relationships. *Sociology of Education, 72*(1), 37–53.

Laurenson, P., McDermott, K., Sadleir, K., & Meade, D. (2015). From national policy to classroom practice: Promoting reading for pleasure in post-primary English classrooms. *English in Education, 49*(1), 4–24.

Leander, K. M., & Hollet, T. (2013). Designing new spaces for learning. In P. J. Dunston, S. K. Fullerton, C. C. Bates, P. M. Stecker, M. W. Cole, A. H. Hall, D. Herro & K. N. Headley (Eds.), *62nd yearbook of the Literacy Research Association* (pp. 29–42). Altamonte Springs, FL: Literacy Research Association.

Leander, K. M., & Lovvorn, J. F. (2006). Literacy networks: Following the circulation of texts, bodies, and objects in the schooling and online gaming of one youth. *Cognition and Instruction, 24*(3), 291–340.

Leander, K. M., Phillips, N. C., & Taylor, K. H. (2010). The changing social spaces of learning: Mapping new mobilities. *Review of Research in Education, 34*, 329–393.

Lee, A., & Pang, A. (2000). *No other city: The Ethos anthology of urban poetry*. Singapore: Ethos.

Lee, C. D. (2001). Is October Brown Chinese? A cultural modeling activity system for underachieving students. *American Educational Research Journal, 38*(1), 97–141.

Lee, K. Y. (2011). Speech by Mr Lee Kuan Yew, former minister mentor and current senior advisor to Government of Singapore Investment Corporation at the launch of the English Language Institute of Singapore (ELIS) on Tuesday, 6 September 2011, at the Marina Bay Sands Expo and Convention Centre. Retrieved March 2, 2015, from Ministry of Education http://www.moe.gov.sg/media/speeches/2011/09/06/speech-by-mr-lee-kuan-yew-at-elis-launch.php

Lee, M., Wright, E., & Walker, A. (2016). The emergence of elite International Baccaureate Diploma programme schools in China: A "skyboxification" perspective. In A. Koh & J. Kenway (Eds.), *Elite schools: Multiple geographies of privilege* (pp. 50–69). Singapore: Routledge.

Lee, V. (2011). Becoming the reading mentors our adolescents deserve: Developing a successful sustained silent reading programme. *Journal of Adolescent and Adult Literacy, 55*(3), 209–218.

Lefebvre, H. (1991). *The production of space* (D. Nicholson-Smith, Trans.). Cambridge, MA: Blackwell.

Leyl, S. (2014, February 27). How do Singapore's poor families get by. *BBC News*. Retrieved from http://www.bbc.com/news/world-asia-26349689

Lien Centre for Social Innovation. (2015). *A handbook on inequality, poverty and unmet social needs in Singapore*. Singapore: Lien Centre for Social Innovation.

Liew, M. (1981). *The design of secondary schools*. Paris, France: UNESCO.

Lim, L. (2014). Ideology, rationality and reproduction in education: A critical discourse analysis. *Discourse: Studies in the cultural politics of education, 35*(1), 61–76.

Loertscher, D. V., Preddy, L., & Derry, B. (2013). Makerspaces in the school library learning commons and the uTEC Maker Model. *Teacher Librarian, 41*(2), 48–51.

Loh, C. E. (2012). Global and national imaginings: Deparochialising the IBDP English A1 curriculum. *Changing English, 19*(2), 221–235.

Loh, C. E. (2013a). Mapping the development of literature education in Singapore Secondary Schools from late-1990s to 2013. In C. E. Loh, D. Yeo & W. M. Liew (Eds.), *Teaching literature in Singapore Secondary Schools* (pp. 20–33). Singapore: Pearson.

Loh, C. E. (2013b). Singaporean boys constructing global literate selves through their reading practices in and out of school. *Anthropology and Education Quarterly, 44*(1), 38–57.

Loh, C. E. (2014, June 3). School libraries levelling playing field. *The Straits Times*. Retrieved from http://www.straitstimes.com/opinion/school-libraries-levelling-playing-field

Loh, C. E. (2015a). Building a reading culture in a Singapore school: Identifying spaces for change through a socio-spatial approach. *Changing English, 22*(2), 209–221.

Loh, C. E. (2015b). Mapping library spaces: Measuring the effectiveness of school libraries using a socio-spatial approach. *The School Librarian, 63*(2), 78–80.

Loh, C. E. (2016a). Elite schoolboys becoming global citizens: Examining the practice of habitus. In A. Koh & J. Kenway (Eds.), *Elite schools: Multiple geographies of privilege* (pp. 70–86). New York: Routledge.

Loh, C. E. (2016b). In remembrance of reading. *Biblioasia, 12*(1), 46–53.

Loh, C. E. (2016c). Levelling the reading gap: A socio-spatial study of school libraries and reading in Singapore. *Literacy, 50*(1), 3–13. doi: 10.1111/lit.12067

Loh, C. E., & Liew, W. M. (2016). Voices from the ground: The emotional labour of English teachers' work. *Teaching and Teacher Education, 55*, 267–278.

Loh, K. K. J. (2009). Teaching modeling: Its impact on an extensive reading program. *Reading in a Foreign Language, 21*(2), 93–118.

Lois, W. (2014). A comment on class productions in elite secondary schools in twenty-first-century global context. *Globalisation, Societies and Education, 12*(2), 309–320.

Long, E. (1993). Textual interpretation as collective action. In J. Boyarin (Ed.), *The ethnography of reading* (pp. 180–211). Berkeley, CA: University of California Press.

Lonsdale, M. (2003). *Impact of school libraries on student achievement: A review of the research*. Victoria, Australia: Australian Council for Educational Research.

Lucero, A. (2010). Dora's program: A constructively marginalized paraeducator and her developmental biliteracy program. *Anthropology and Education Quarterly, 41*(2), 126–143.

Luke, A. (1988). *Literacy, textbooks and ideology*. London: The Falmer Press.

Luke, A. (2000). Critical literacy in Australia: A matter of context and standpoint. *Journal of Adolescent and Adult Literacy, 43*(5), 448–461.

Luke, A. (2004). Teaching after the market: From commodity to cosmopolitan. *Teachers College Record, 106*(7), 1422–1443.

Luke, A., & Carrington, V. (2004). Globalization, literacy, curriculum practice. In T. Grainger (Ed.), *The RoutledgeFalmer reader in language & literacy* (pp. 52–65). New York: RoutledgeFalmer.

Luke, A., & Freebody, P. (1997a). Critical literacy and the question of normativity: An introduction. In S. Muspratt, A. Luke & P. Freebody (Eds.), *Constructing critical literacies: Teaching and learning textual practices* (pp. 1–18). Cresskill, NJ: Hamptom.

Luke, A., & Freebody, P. (1997b). Shaping the social practices of reading. In S. Muspratt, A. Luke & P. Freebody (Eds.), *Constructing critical literacies: Teaching and learning textual practice* (pp. 185–225). Cresskill, NJ: Hampton.

Luke, A., & Goldstein, T. (2006). Building intercultural capital: A response to Rogers, Marshall, and Tyson. *Reading Research Quarterly, 41*(2), 202–224.

Lupton, R. (2005). Social justice and school improvement: Improving the quality of schooling in the poorest neighbourhoods. *British Educational Research Journal, 31*(5), 589–604.

Mahony, P., & Hextall, I. (2000). *Reconstructing teaching: Standards, performance, and accountability*. New York: RoutledgeFalmer.

Maira, S. (2004). Imperial feelings: Youth culture, citizenship, and globalization. In M. M. Suárez-Orozco & D. B. Qin-Hillard (Eds.), *Globalization: Culture and education in the new millennium* (pp. 203–234). Berkeley, CA: University of California Press.

Maira, S., & Soep, E. (2005). Introduction. In S. Maira & E. Soep (Eds.), *Youthscapes: The popular, the national, the global* (pp. xv–xx). Philadelphia, PA: University of Pennsylvania Press.

Majid, S., Chaudhry, A., Foo, S., & Logan, E. (2002). *Developing 21st century school media resource libraries for Singapore: An assessment and proposal from a library and information science education taskforce.* Paper presented at the international Association of School Librarianship, Malaysia.

Makatche, K., & Oberlin, J. U. (2011). Building a culture of reading. *School Lirbary Monthly, 28*, 12–14.

Martel, Y. (2001). *The Life of Pi*. New York: Knopf Canada

Massey, D. (2005). *For space*. London: Sage.

Mathews, M. (2016, April 29). In good social policy, every child matters. *The Straits Times*. Retrieved from http://www.straitstimes.com/opinion/in-good-social-policy-every-child-matters

Maynard, S., Mackay, S., & Smyth, F. (2008). A survey of young people's reading in England: Borrowing and choosing books. *Journal of Librarianship and Information Science, 40*(4), 239–253.

McCarthey, S. J., & Moje, E. B. (2002). Conversations: Identity matters. *Reading Research Quarterly, 37*(2), 228–238.

McKechnie, L., & Rothbauer, P. M. (2006). *Reading matters: What the research reveals about reading, libraries and community*. Westport, CT: Libraries Unlimited.

McNamee, S. J., & Miller, R. K. J. (2004). *The meritocracy myth*. Oxford, UK: Rowman & Littlefield.

Meadmore, D., & Meadmore, P. (2004). The boundlessness of performativity in elite Australian schools. *Discourse: Studies in the Cultural Politics of Education, 25*(3), 375–387.

Meek, M. (1982). *Learning to read*. London: The Bodley Head.

Merga, M. K. (2015). Access to books in the home and adolescent engagement in recreational book reading: Considerations for secondary educators. *English in Education, 49*(3), 197–214.

Millard, E. (1997). *Differently literate: Boys, girls and the schooling of literacy*. London: The Falmer Press.

Mills, K. A., & Comber, B. (2015). Socio-spatial approaches to literacy studies. In J. Roswell & K. Pahl (Eds.), *The Routledge handbook of literacy studies* (pp. 91–103). New York: Routledge.

Ministry of Education. (2008). *Introduction: The stellar vision*. Retrieved December 31, 2014, from http://www.stellarliteracy.sg/cos/o.x?c=/wbn/pagetree&func=view&rid=1143645

Ministry of Education. (2010). *English syllabus 2010: Primary & Secondary (Express/Normal [Academic])*. Singapore: MOE.

Ministry of Education. (2012). *Literature in English teaching syllabus 2013 (Lower and Upper Secondary*. Singapore: MOE.

Ministry of Education. (2013). *Parlimentary replies: Government expenditure on education* [Press release]. Retrieved from http://www.moe.gov.sg/media/parliamentary-replies/2013/10/government-expenditure-on-education.php

Ministry of Education. (2015). *21st century competencies*. Retrieved June 9, 2016, from https://www.moe.gov.sg/education/education-system/21st-century-competencies

Mitchell, J. C. (1983). Case and situation analysis. *Sociological Review, 31*(2), 187–211.

Moje, E. B. (2004). Powerful spaces: Racing the out-of-school literacy spaces of Latino/a youth. In K. M. Leander & M. Sheehy (Eds.), *Spatializing literacy research and practice* (pp. 15–38). New York: Peter Lang.

Moje, E. B., Overby, M., Tysvaer, N., & Morris, K. (2008). The complex world of adolescent literacy: Myths, motivations, and mysteries. *Harvard Educational Review, 78*(1), 107–157.

Mokhtar, I. A. (2003). *Evaluation of the collaborative relationship between teachers and school librarians in Singapore.* (Master of Science (Information Studies)), Nanyang Technological University, Singapore.

Mokhtar, I. A., & Majid, S. (2005). Use of school libraries by teachers in Singapore schools. *Library Review, 54*(2), 108–118.

Moll, L. C., Amanti, C., Neff, D., & Gonzalez, N. (1992). Funds of knowledge for teaching: Using a qualitative approach to connect homes and classrooms. *Theory into Practice, 31*(2), 133–141.

Moss, G. (2007). *Literacy and gender: Researching texts, contexts and readers.* London: Routledge.

Nair, P., Fielding, R., & Lackney, J. (2009). *The language of school design: Design patterns for 21st century schools.* Minneapolis, MN: DesignShare.

National Arts Council. (2015). *2015 National literary reading and writing survey.* Singapore: National Arts Council.

National Endowment for the Arts. (2007). *To read or not to read: A question of national consequence.* Washington, DC: National Endowment for the Arts.

Nespor, J. (1997). *Tangled up in school: Politics, space, bodies and signs in the educational process.* Mahwah, NJ: Lawrence Erlbaum.

Neuman, S. B., & Celano, D. (2001). Access to print in low-income and middle-income communities: An ecological study of four neighbourhood. *Reading Research Quarterly, 36*(1), 8–26.

Neuman, S. B., & Celano, D. (2012a). *Giving our children a fighting chance: Poverty, literacy, and the development of information capital.* New York: Teachers College Press.

Neuman, S. B., & Celano, D. (2012b). Worlds apart: One city, two libraries, and ten years of watching inequality grow. *American Educator, 36*(3), 13–23.

New London Group, T. (1996). A pedagogy of multiliteracies: Designing social futures. *Harvard Educational Review, 66*(1), 60–87.

Ng, I. Y. H. (2014). Education and intergenerational mobility in Singapore. *Educational Review, 66*(3), 362–376.

Ng, J. (2013, March 3). Reigniting the spark of literature. *The Straits Times.*

Ng, S. M., & Sullivan, C. (2001). The Singapore reading and English aquisition program. *International Journal of Educational Research, 35,* 157–167.

Nichols, S. (2011). Young children's literacy in the activity space of the library: A geo-semiotic investigation. *Journal of Early Childhood Literacy, 11*(2), 164–189.

Nichols, S. (2014). Geosemitotics. In P. Albers, T., F. Holbrook & A. Seely (Eds.), *New methods of literacy research* (pp. 177–192). New York: Routledge.

Nogueira, M. A. (2010). A revisited theme: Middle classes and the school. In M. W. Apple, S. J. Ball & L. A. Gandin (Eds.), *The Routledge international handbook of the sociology of education* (pp. 253–263). New York: Routledge.

Nussbaum, M. C. (1997). *Cultivating humanity: A classical defense of reform in liberal education.* Cambridge: Harvard University Press.

Oakes, J., & Lipton, M. (2013). Schools that shock the conscience: Williams v. California and the struggle for education on equal terms fifty years after Brown. *Berkeley Journal of Gender, Law & Justice, 19*(2), 234–258.

OECD. (2010a). *PISA 2009 results: Learning to learn: Student engagement, strategies and practices, volume III*. Paris, France: OECD.
OECD. (2010b). *Singapore: Rapid improvement followed by strong performance*. Paris, France: OECD.
OECD. (2011). *Strong performers and successful reformers in education: Lessons from PISA for the United States*. Paris, France: OECD.
OECD. (2013). *Key findings from the Teaching and Learning International Survey (TALIS)*. Amsterdam, The Netherlands: Organisation for Economic Cooperation and Development.
Olds, K., & Thrift, N. (2005). Cultures on the brink: Reengineering the soul of capitalism: On a global scale. In A. Ong & S. J. Collier (Eds.), *Global assemblages: Technology, politics, and ethics as anthropological problems* (pp. 270–290). Oxford, UK: Blackwell.
Ong, A. (1999). *Flexible citizenship: The cultural logics of transnationality*. Durham and London: Duke University Press.
Pahl, K. (2008). Tracing habitus in texts: Narratives of loss, displacement and migration in homes. In J. Albright & A. Luke (Eds.), *Pierre Bourdieu and literacy education* (pp. 187–208). New York: Routledge.
Peterson, R. A., & Kern, R. M. (1996). Changing highbrow taste: From snob to omnivore. *American Sociological Review, 61*(5), 900–907.
Piketty, T. (2014). *Capital in the twenty-first century* (A. Goldhammer, Trans.). Cambridge, MA: Belknap.
Poon, A. (2007). The politics of pragmatism: Some issues in the teaching of literature in Singapore. *Changing English, 14*(1), 51–59.
Pressley, M., & Allington, R. L. (2015). *Reading instruction that works: The case for balanced teaching*. New York: Guilford.
Radway, J. A. (1997). *A feeling for books: The book-of-the-month club, literary taste, and middle-class desire*. Chapel Hill and London: University of North Carolina Press.
Ramesh, S. (2011, January 24). MM Lee says students' background plays a role, *Channel News Asia*.
Reardon, S. F. (2013). The widening income achievement gap. *Educational Leadership, 70*(8), 10–16.
Reay, D. (2004). "It's all becoming habitus": Beyond the habitual use of habitus in educational research. *British Journal of Sociology of Education, 25*(4), 431–444.
Reay, D. (2006a). Compounding inequalities: Gender and class in education. In C. Skelton, B. Francis & L. Smulyan (Eds.), *The Sage handbook of gender and education* (pp. 339–349). Thousand Oaks, CA: Sage.
Reay, D. (2006b). The zombie stalking English schools: Social class and educational inequality. *British Journal of Educational Studies, 54*(3), 288–307.
Reay, D. (2013). The white middle classes and urban comprehensive schools: Ambivalences and anxieties of privilege. In C. Maxwell & P. Aggleton (Eds.), *Privilege, agency and affect: Understanding the production and effects of action* (pp. 167–184). London: Palgrave MacMillan.
Reay, D., Crozier, G., & James, D. (2013). *White middle-class identities and urban schooling*. New York: Palgrave MacMillan.
Reay, D., David, M., & Ball, S. J. (2001). Making a difference? Institutional habituses and higher education choice. *Sociological Research Online, 5*(4), 4126–4142.
Reich, R. B. (1991). *The work of nations*. New York: Vintage Books.

Resnik, J. (2008). The construction of the global worker through international education. In J. Resnik (Ed.), *The production of educational knowledge in the global era* (pp. 147–168). Rotterdam, The Netherlands: Sense.
Rex, L. A. (2001). The remaking of a high school reader. *Reading Research Quarterly, 36*(3), 288–314.
Richards, I. A. (1929). *Practical criticism.* New York: Harcourt Brace.
Rizvi, F. (2008). Education and its cosmopolitan possibilities. In B. Lingard, J. Nixon & S. Ranson (Eds.), *Transforming learning in schools and communities: The remaking of education for a cosmopolitan society* (pp. 101–116). London: Continuum.
Robertson, S. L. (2010). "Spatilzing" the sociology of education: Stand-points, entry-points, vantage-points. In M. W. Apple, S. J. Ball & L. A. Gandin (Eds.), *The Routledge international handbook of the sociology of education* (pp. 15–26). New York: Routledge.
Robin Hood. (n.d.). *The L!brary initiative.* Retrieved November 15, 2015, from https://www.robinhood.org/initiatives/library
Rosales, J. (n.d.). *Checking out: Budget hawks see library programs as an easy cut, but what's the cost to student achievement.* Retrieved July 8, 2016, from http://www.nea.org/home/43952.htm
Rosenblatt, L. M. (1994). *The reader, the text, the poem: The transactional theory of the literary work.* Carbondale, IL: Southern Illinois University Press.
Rosenblatt, L. M. (1995). *Literature as exploration.* New York: Modern Language Association.
Ross, C. S., McKechnie, L. E. F., & Routhbauer, P. M. (2006). *Reading matters: What the research reveals about reading, libraries, and communities.* Westport, CT: Libraries Unlimited.
Ross, T. J. (2006). School libraries and evidence-based practice: An integrated approach to evidence. *School Libraries Worldwide, 12*(2), 31–37.
Salberg, P., Ravitch, D., & Hargreaves, A. (2014). *Finnish lessons 2.0: What can the world learn from educational change in Finland?* (2nd ed.). New York: Teachers College Press.
Samuels, S. J., & Farstrup, A. E. (2011). *What research has to say about reading instruction* (4th ed.). Newark, DE: Internationl Reading Association.
Samuels, S. J., & Wu, Y.-C. (2001). *How the amount of time spent on independent reading affects reading achievement.* Minneapolis, MN: University of Minnesota Press.
Savage, M., Devine, F., Cunningham, N., Taylor, M., Li, Y., Hjellbrekke, J.,Le Roux, B., Friedman, S., & Miles, A. (2013). A new model of social class: Findings from the BBC's great British class survey experiment. *Sociology, 47*(2), 219–250.
Schmidt, S. J. (2015). A queer arrangement of school: Using spatiality to understand inequity. *Jounal of Curriculum Studies, 47*(2), 253–273.
Schneider, A. (2005). "Jackie Chan is nobody, and so am I": Juvenile fan culture and the construction of transnational male identity in the tamil diaspora. In S. Maira & E. Soep (Eds.), *Youthscapes: The popular, the national, the global* (pp. 137–154). Philadelphia, PA: University of Pennsylvania Press.
Scollon, R., & Scollon, S. W. (2003). *Discourses in place: Language in the material world.* New York: Routledge.
Sharpe, L., & Gopinathan, S. (2002). After effectiveness: New directions in the Singapore school system? *Journal of Educational Policy, 17*(2), 151–166.

Sheehy, M. (2004). Between a thick and a thin place. In K. M. Leander & M. Sheeny (Eds.), *Spatializing literacy research and practice* (pp. 91–114). New York: Peter Lang.

Shilling, C., & Cousins, F. (1990). Social use of the school library: The colonisation and regulation of educational space. *British Journal of Sociology of Education, 11*(4), 411–430.

Silver, R. E. (2005). The discourse of linguistic capital: Language and economic policy planning in Singapore. *Language Policy, 4*(1), 47–66.

Silver, R. E., Curdt-Christiansen, X., Wright, S., & Stinson, M. (2013). Working through the layers: Curriculum implementation in language education. In Z. Deng, S. Gopinathan & C. Lee (Eds.), *Globalization and the Singapore curriculum: From policy to classroom* (pp. 151–168). London: Springer.

Simpson, A. (1996). Fictions and facts: An investigation of the reading practices of girls and boys. *English Education, 28*(4), 268–279.

Singapore Examinations and Assessment Board & Cambridge International Examinations. (2014). *Literature in English: Higher 2 (2016) (Syllabus 9748)*. Singapore: MOE & UCLES.

Smith, C., Constantino, R., & Krashen, S. D. (1997). Differences in print environment for children in Beverly Hills, Compton and Watts. *Emergency Librarian, 24*(4), 8–9.

Smith, F. (1988). *Joining the literacy club: Further essays into education*. Portsmouth, NH: Heinemann.

Smith, M. W., & Wilhelm, J. D. (2002). *Reading don't fix no chevys: Literacy in the lives of young men*. Portsmouth, NH: Heinemann.

Soja, E. W. (1989). *Postmodern geographies: The reassertion of space in critical social theory*. London: Verso.

Soja, E. (2009). The city and spatial justice. *Justice Spatiale/Spatial Justice, 1*. http://www.jssj.org/wp-content/uploads/2012/12/JSSJ1-1en4.pdf

Soler, J., & Openshaw, R. (2006). *Literacy crises and reading policies: Children still can't read*. New York: Routledge.

Solsken, J. W. (1993). *Literacy, gender, and work in families and in schools*. Norwood, NJ: Ablex.

Speak Good English Movement. (n.d.). Speak Good English Movement. Retrieved March 28, 2016, from http://goodenglish.org.sg

Spolsky, B. (2012). Language testing and language management. In G. Fulcher & F. Davidson (Eds.), *The Routledge handbook of language testing* (pp. 495–505). New York: Routledge.

Stanovich, K. E. (1986). Matthew effects in reading: Some consequences of individual differences in the acquisition of literacy. *Reading Research Quarterly, 22*, 306–407.

Street, B. V. (1984). *Literacy in theory and practice*. Cambridge, UK: Cambridge University Press.

Street, B. V. (1993). Introduction: The new literacy studies. In B. V. Street (Ed.), *Cross-cultural approaches to literacy* (pp. 1–21). Cambridge: Cambridge University Press.

Sullivan, A., & Brown, M. (2013). Social inequalities in cognitive scores at age 16: The role of reading. *CLS Working Paper 2013/10*. London: Centre for Longitudinal Studies.

Sullivan, A., Ketende, S., & Joshi, H. (2013). Social class and inequalities in early cognitive scores. *Sociology, 47*(6), 1187–1206.

Sullivan, M. L. (2015). *High impact school library spaces: Envisioning new school library concepts.* Santa Barbara, CA: Libraries Unlimited.

Sumara, D. J. (1998). Fictionalizing acts: Reading and the making of identity. *Theory into practice, 37*(3), 203–210.

Swartz, D. (1997). *Culture and power: The sociology of Pierre Bourdieu.* Chicago, IL: University of Chicago Press.

Tan, C. N. (2003). *School media resource libraries in Singapore: An assessment and potential developments.* (Master of Science [Information Studies]), Nanyang Technological University, Singapore.

Tan, E. S. (2004). *Does class matter? Social stratification and orientations in Singapore.* Singapore: World Scientific.

Tan, E. S. (2015). *Class and social orientations: Key findings from the social stratification suvey 2011.* Singapore: Institute of Policy Studies.

Tan, J. (2010). Education in Singapore: Sorting them out? In T. Chong (Ed.), *Management of success: Singapore revisited* (pp. 288–308). Singapore: Institute of Southeast Asian Studies.

Tan, J., & Gopinathan, S. (2000). Educational reform for the 21st century. *NIRA review, 7*(3), 5–10.

Tan, K. P. (2008). Meritocracy and elitism in a global city: Ideological shifts in Singapore. *International Political Science Review, 29*(1), 7–27.

Taylor, C. (1989). *Sources of the self: The making of the modern identity.* Cambridge, MA: Harvard University Press.

Teh, L. W. (2014). Singapore's performance in PISA: Levelling up the long tail. In S. K. Lee, W. O. Lee & E. L. Low (Eds.), *Educational policy innovations: Levelling up and sustaining educational achievement* (pp. 71–83). Amsterdam, The Netherlands: Springer.

Teng, A. (2015a, July 4). Better educated parents with higher incomes spend more. *The Straits Times.* Retrieved from http://www.straitstimes.com/singapore/education/better-educated-parents-with-higher-incomes-spend-more

Teng, A. (2015b, August 4). Raffles Institution now a "middle-class" school, says principal. *The Straits Times.* Retrieved from http://www.straitstimes.com/singapore/education/raffles-institution-now-a-middle-class-school-says-principal

Teng, A. (2016, April 8). PSLE aggregate score to be scrapped, DSA to be reviewed: Education changes at a glance. *The Straits Times.* Retrieved from http://www.straitstimes.com/singapore/education/psle-aggregate-score-to-be-scrapped-dsa-to-be-reviewed-education-changes-at-a

Teo, Y. Y. (2016, March 10). Why low-income parents may make "poor choices", Opinion Editorial. *The Straits Times.* Retrieved from http://www.straitstimes.com/opinion/why-low-income-parents-may-make-poor-choices

Thrupp, M., & Tomlinson, S. (2005). Introduction: Education policy, social justice and "complex hope". *British Educational Research Journal, 31*(5), 549–556.

Tobin, K., Kincheloe, J. L., & Patron, M.-C. (2012). *Legacy of the baby boomers or the French social system: Issues of equality and brain drain.* Rotterdam, The Netherlands: Sense.

Todd, R. J., & Kuhlthau, C. C. (2005). Student learning through Ohio school libraries, Part 1: How effective school libraries help students. *School Libraries Worldwide, 11*(11), 63–88.

Tomlinson, J. (1999). *Globalization and culture.* Chicago, IL: University of Chicago Press.

Tsai, J. W. (2001). *Refining roles and competencies of library coordinators in Singapore secondary schools.* (Master of Science [Information Studies]), Nanyang Technological University, Singapore.

Tuan, Y.-F. (1974). *Topophilia.* New York: Columbia University Press.

Tuan, Y.-F. (1977). *Space and place.* Minneapolis, MN: University of Minnesota Press.

Twomey, S. (2007). Reading "woman": Book club pedagogies & the literary imagination. *Journal of Adolescent and Adult Literacy, 50*(5), 398–407.

Unknown Author. (1995, October 7). Brighter students should study literature: Minister. *The Straits Times.* Retrieved from http://eresources.nlb.gov.sg/newspapers/digitised/briefcase.aspx.

Valencia, R. R. (2010). *Dismantling contemporary deficit thinking: Educational thought and practice.* New York: Routledge.

Velayutham, S. (2007). *Responding to globalization: Nation, culture, and identity in Singapore.* Singapore: Institute of Southeast Asian Studies.

Vidovich, L., & Yap, M. S. (2008). Global-local dynamics in expanding school choice in Singapore. In M. Forsey, S. Davis & G. Walford (Eds.), *The globalisation of school choice* (pp. 209–230). Oxford, UK: Symposium.

Walkerdine, V. (1990). *Schoolgirl fictions.* London: Verso.

Wallace, C. (2003). Local literacies and global literacy. In S. Goodman, T. Lillis, J. Maybin & N. Mercer (Eds.), *Language, literacy and education: A reader* (pp. 89–101). London: Trentham Books.

Warshauer, M. (2007). The paradoxical future of digital learning. *Learning Inquiry, 1*, 1–49.

Waters, J. L. (2006). Geographies of cultural capital: Education, international migration and family strategies between Hong Kong and Canada. *Transactions of the Institute of British Geographers, 31*, 179–192.

Weaver-Hightower, M. (2003). The "boy turn" in research on gender and education. *Review of Educational Research, 73*, 471–498.

Weis, L., & Dolby, N. (2012). *Social class and education: Global perspectives.* New York: Routledge.

Wejrowski, K., & McRae, M. (2013). Developing a culture of readers through effective library planning. *Knowledge Quest, 42*(1), 38–43.

Wilhelm, J. D. (2016). Recognizing the power of pleasure: What engaged adolescent readers get from their free-choice reading, and how teachers can leverage this for all. *Australian Journal of Language and Literacy, 39*(1), 30–41.

Williams, R. (1977). *Marxism and literature.* Oxford, UK: Oxford University Press.

Willis, P. E. (1975). *Learning to labour: How working class kids get working class jobs.* Birmingham, UK: Centre for Contemporary Cultural Studies.

Windle, J., & Nogueira, M. A. (2015). The role of internationalisation in the schooling of Brazilian elites: Distinction between two factions. *Discourse: Studies in the Cultural Politics of Education, 36*(1), 174–192.

Windle, J., & Stratton, G. (2012). Equity for sale: Ethical consumption in a school-choice regime. *Discourse: Studies in the Cultural Politics of Education, 34*(2), 202–213.

Wolf, J. M., & Bokhorst-Heng, W. D. (2008). Policies of promise and practices of limit: Singapore's literacy education policy landscape and its impact on one school programme. *Educational Research in Policy and Practice, 7*, 151–164.

Worthy, J., Moorman, M., & Turner, M. (1999). What Johnny likes to read is hard to find in school. *Reading Research Quarterly, 34*(1), 12–27.

Ye, R., & Nylander, E. (2015). The transactional track: State sponsorship and Singapore's Oxbridge elite. *Discourse: Studies in the Cultural Politics of Education, 36*(1), 11–33.

Yin, R. K. (2003). *Case study research: Design & methods* (3rd ed.). Thousand Oaks, CA: Sage.

Young, J. P., & Bozo, W. G. (2003). Boys will be boys, or will they? Literacy and masculinities. *Reading Research Quarterly, 36*(3), 316–325.

Index

academic achievement 12–13, 28, 33, 39–40, 71–2, 85, 94–5, 99, 103; achievement gap 3; low achievement 5, 25, 41, 83, 85–6, 103
access: education, access to 5, 17, 48, 72; equitable access 4, 9, 13–14, 72; knowledge, access to 8, 77, 100; physical access 72, 75, 82; reading, access to 1–2, 9, 14, 98; relative access 72, 97; resources, access to 8–9, 13–14, 18, 25, 33, 36–7, 40–1, 45, 66–7, 71–3, 89–94, 97–8, 100; space, access to 70, 73, 75, 82
accountability 6, 23, 39–41, 43
adolescent 6, 9, 25–6, 29, 39, 41–3, 71, 89, 91–2, 95, 97
aesthetic 40, 50, 61
affective *see* emotion
agency 2, 10–11, 32, 72, 90, 101–2
alignment 13, 15, 65, 70, 103; alignment of curriculum 21, 61; alignment of policy 46, 48, 51; alignment of practices 34, 54, 58, 74
assessment 4, 16, 51, 52–3, 56, 61, 63, 94, 100–3; oral 52–3, 56, 61; research 53; traditional 52, 100; written 52–3, 61
autonomy, student *see* agency

Ball, Stephen 3–4, 14, 32, 51
beliefs 1–3, 27, 50, 63, 94, 103
book recommendations 27, 29, 31, 43, 57
bookshop 28–9, 31, 57, 71, 84, 96
Bourdieu, Pierre 2–3, 10–13, 15, 21, 24, 27, 29, 47, 51–3, 57, 68, 85, 90

capital 3, 8; cultural (*see* cultural capital); economic 12, 33, 47; human 8, 15–16, 48; information 8, 47, 100; linguistic 8, 42, 51, 63; social 8, 12–13, 33, 47, 61; symbolic 12–13, 64
Certeau, Michel de 2, 10, 61, 68
Cherland, Meredith 2, 31, 33, 34
cognitive perspectives on reading 2
Collins & Blot 2, 9–11, 47, 50–1, 101
concerted cultivation 8, 33, 47
confidence 21–2, 42, 51–2, 55–60, 96
consumption 52, 55, 57, 60–1
conversations 7, 10, 28, 34–6, 43, 53, 55–6
cosmopolitans 46–52, 60; selective cosmopolitans 47; strategic cosmopolitanism 63
creativity 17, 45, 48, 64, 103
credentials 3, 12, 45–6, 48
criticality 48, 59, 103
critical reading 32, 57–8, 60, 62, 93, 100–3
critical thinking 17, 60, 63–5, 92, 103
crossings 5, 54, 60
cultural capital: academic achievement and cultural capital 13, 33, 47–8; cosmopolitans and cultural capital 46–7; curriculum as cultural capital 50–1, 53; distinction and cultural capital 63; embodied cultural capital 12, 47–8, 60; English language as cultural capital 49–50; institutionalised cultural capital 12, 47; intercultural capital 61–3, 101; parental cultural capital 6, 8; reading as cultural capital 2, 4, 12, 22, 32–3, 42, 47, 96; situated cultural capital 13; social class and cultural capital 3–4, 47; social mobility and cultural

capital 13; specified, embodied, and institutionalised cultural capital 12–13
cultural omnivores 52, 58
culture: high 4, 33, 52, 59–60; popular 42, 60, 91
curriculum 43, 50–1, 61–2; core 56; enacted 54, 57, 64; hidden 64, 100; national 50–1, 64; official 23, 50–1, 54, 62–3; school 29, 48, 51–4, 59, 62–3; skills-oriented 50, 63, 65, 94, 101, 103

deficit mentality 4, 33, 66–7, 90–2, 103
De Graaf, N.D. ; 4, 6, 13, 33
differentiation: differentiated curriculum 100; differentiated space 67; differentiation and inequalities 66; differentiation in education 17, 49, 60, 64, 67; differentiation of English curriculum 50
discourses: community 66; competing 13–14, 68, 93; dominant 14, 16, 43, 66–8, 72, 74, 93, 104; institutional 11, 51–2, 66, 95; macro-discourse 1, 15; meritocracy, discourse of 17, 90; national 11, 18, 66; neoliberal 14, 45–6; official 11, 26, 40, 74, 77, 95; policy discourse 24; public 45, 49, 51; reading, discourse of 31, 73; situational 11; space, discourse of 73; unofficial 77
discrimination *see* marginalised
disposition 5, 11–12, 26–7, 49, 52, 57–62, 65, 70, 89, 91; acquisition of 40, 46–7, 63, 85, 100–1, 103
distinction 21, 47, 51–2, 57, 59–60, 63

ease 54, 57, 60
ecology 2, 7, 9, 14, 21
economic needs 16, 17, 45, 51, 62
economic success 3, 16, 45
educational advancement 65
educational advantage 8, 13, 32–3, 47, 102–3; accumulation of educational advantage 4, 47–8, 54
educational attainment: educational success 3, 16; parents' education 4, 6, 17, 21, 33, 46
educational disadvantage 4, 10, 33, 35, 41, 86, 97; addressing educational disadvantage 5, 9, 14, 72, 87, 98, 103
educational qualifications 12, 47, 93

elite 3; class practices 22, 46, 52, 60; elitism 16; schooling/students 22, 45–52, 57, 60, 62–4, 70, 86, 101
emotion 37, 66, 70–1, 73–5, 83–4, 87, 91–9
engaged reading 6, 39, 95–6, 103–4
English fluency 22–3, 49–51, 53, 57, 63–5, 92
English language teaching 50
enjoyment of reading 26, 31–2, 35, 40, 42, 71, 96
entertainment 12, 28–9, 31, 59, 61, 96
equity/inequity: education equity 3–5, 62, 88, 92–3; equal opportunity 41, 64, 68; systemic inequities 5, 67
ethnographic 7, 9, 14, 21, 64
examination 17–18, 21, 23, 29, 50, 52–3, 62, 94; examination-oriented 6, 43, 51, 56, 64, 90, 94–5, 100, 102, 103
experiences of reading 7, 9–10, 35, 37, 39, 42, 71–3, 87, 89, 96–8
exposure to reading 7–8, 18, 33, 43, 54, 71, 96
extensive reading (Sustained Silent Reading, Book Flood, Independent reading) 23, 35, 38, 39, 43, 71, 75, 95

field 12–13, 15
flexibility 48, 61–2, 65, 101; flexible reading 35, 54, 58, 60–1, 63, 65, 85
"flow" 26, 91

gender 33–5
generative possibilities 12
global/globalization 16, 22, 46, 101; global citizens 22, 47, 52, 62, 65, 77, 101; global English-Speaking markets 22, 49, 63; global literate citizens 45–8, 54, 57, 60–5; international/global markets/economy 4–5, 15, 45–6, 48–51, 63–5

habitus 11–13, 27, 33, 36, 41, 51, 90–1, 93; institutional/school 42, 48, 51–2, 57, 60, 63–4, 93; national 48, 51, 63–4; personal 48, 60, 93
Harvey, David 2, 3, 14, 67, 72
Heath, Shirley Brice 7, 9–10, 12, 25, 28, 51, 91, 101
hegemony/hegemonic 67–8, 93

Index

Holland, D. 11, 12, 90
home language 20, 22–3, 102

identity: self-definition 3, 26, 36; self-making 10–11, 27, 46–8, 55, 62; self-projection 48, 50, 54, 63; subjectivity 10–11, 51–2
ideology 7, 16, 29, 31, 50–1, 66–70, 73, 86, 90, 101
include/exclude 12, 70, 72, 101–2
income: elasticity of 16; high 3–4, 18, 62, 64, 70; inequality 3–4, 16, 90, 103; low 3, 4–6, 9, 14–15, 18, 22, 33, 35, 41, 47, 70–3, 83, 86–7, 97–8, 102–3
inquiry-based research 64, 77, 79, 82–4, 86, 100
institution 10, 67; informal 57; institutional certification 13; institutionalised 12, 47, 57
intensive immersion 28, 36, 41, 91
internalisation 55, 60
International Baccalaureate Diploma Programme (IBDP/IBO) 40, 50–7, 62, 74–5, 77, 79
investment 4, 6, 8, 33, 40–1, 45–6; educational investment 4, 48, 101–3
invisible/make visible 24–5, 66, 73, 89
invisible network of resources 25, 27–9, 33, 36, 41, 44, 91

knowledge: core 65; cultural 51, 57, 60, 65, 57–62
knowledge-intensive work 45, 100

language learning 7–8, 22, 47–8, 101; functional approach to 22, 26, 39, 63, 65, 76, 95
Lareau, Annette 4, 8–9, 12, 25, 32–3, 54, 57, 60
learning to read 1, 8, 18, 66, 87, 90, 101
library: public 9, 28–9, 38, 71–2, 84, 96–8, 100; school 41, 70–7, 82–8, 91, 93, 97–100; staff 73, 75, 92, 98–100
lifelong learning 43
literacy: academic 65; basic 48, 63, 100; critical 100–2; critical information 86, 100; cultural 65; events 76; flexible 32, 42, 46, 61, 64; functional 26, 83; glocalised 102; information 77; local 7; neutral 7; norms of 61; rate of 16; school-sanctioned 7, 9–10, 60–2, 65, 87, 103; traditional 1, 47, 60, 102; universal literacy 7
literary: competence 25, 56, 58, 61; literariness 58
literature: Anglophile/Eurocentric 54; canonical 63; postcolonial 54, 63; Singapore 29; study of 22, 43, 50–2, 54–5, 61, 65; translated literature 52; world 52, 54, 58, 62–3
lived experiences 2, 14, 68
local 1–2, 7, 26, 65, 90
lower social class 3, 34, 62

mapping 73–5, 79, 82–3, 86–7, 90, 94, 105
marginalised 4–5, 15, 72, 100
Massey, Doreen 67, 92–3
meritocracy: and competition 45, 94; and efficiency 17, 90; and equality 16, 46, 64–5, 68, 90, 97, 103
middle class 3–5, 7–9, 11–12, 14, 18, 28, 32–3, 41, 46–7, 57, 60–1, 64, 71, 87, 91, 96–7, 102–3
mobility 10; economic mobility 3; global mobility 62; sponsored mobility 47
Moss, Gemma 1, 9, 25, 34–6, 85
motivation 6, 8, 95; affective/emotional 26–7, 98; and choice 40, 43; and engagement 26, 38–9, 42; extrinsic 37; intrinsic motivation 26, 40; and library use 72, 83, 85–6, 99

narratives 67, 93
networks 14, 25, 27, 66, 73, 99
Neuman, Susan B. & Celano, Donna 6, 8, 9, 21, 33, 41, 72, 87, 98, 101
New Literacy Studies 7

OECD see PISA
opportunities 9, 16
other, the 46, 55, 62, 101

parentocracy 4
personality 9, 11, 27, 29
place 2, 10, 14, 46, 61, 65–8, 70–1, 73–4, 76, 84–5, 90, 98, 102–3
policy 12, 90, 92; economic 16–17; educational 1–2, 4–5, 14–18, 46, 49, 51, 64, 68, 94, 97, 99, 103–4; policy-making 1, 4, 14–15, 65, 87, 93, 103

positioning 32, 58, 100
poverty *see* income, low
power 1–2, 10–11, 63, 70, 90; relations 67–8, 70
practices 73–4; class 1, 3, 14, 46; discursive 63; educational 2, 46, 49, 68; home 2, 7, 60, 85, 96; instructional 63; literacy 25, 74, 91, 95, 101; perspectives 2, 10–13, 89; school 2, 53, 57, 60, 73, 103; situated 2, 20, 66, 74, 90; social 1, 15, 21, 27, 43, 67
predispositions 8, 9, 11, 12, 26–7, 33
primary socialisation 11
print-rich environment 18, 25, 29, 32, 37, 41
Programme for International Assessment (PISA) 5, 16

reader 1, 7; avid 84, 97; community of 96; histories 85; 'natural' 33; non-reader 36–8, 87; reluctant 97; struggling 97
reading: boys 31, 33–5, 39; discussion about books 83, 95–6; gap 6; girls 31, 34; independent 6, 39, 95–6; modes of 32, 63; outreach programme 98; performance 6; score 6, 71; strategy 1, 98; tactical 60, 62
reading choices/preferences 25, 28, 31, 34–5, 40, 43, 58, 60, 72, 95–6
reading competence 25, 32, 34–5, 39–42, 92
reading culture 13, 20, 23, 41, 43, 72, 85, 91, 99)
reading for leisure 26–9, 31, 33, 35, 37–8, 41–2, 84
reading for pleasure 39–42, 57, 87, 95–6
reading habits 4, 6, 8, 11, 13, 29, 33–4, 40, 42, 62, 86, 98, 105
reading identity: acquisition/development/construction of reading identity 9, 25, 27–8, 37, 40–1, 44, 89–92; reading identity and cultural capital 47, 51
reading instruction: and functional literacy 26, 39, 41, 43; examination-oriented 6, 18, 87; and intervention 1, 6–7, 25, 27, 35, 67, 86, 88, 90, 93, 98

reading mediator/model 7, 9, 33, 36, 42, 70–1, 82, 91, 95–6
reading practices 2, 13, 18, 21, 25, 31, 33–4, 40–3, 48, 54, 57, 67, 75, 86–7, 95–6, 105
reading responses 32, 54, 57, 59, 65, 93
Reay, Diane 4, 5, 12, 14, 27, 47, 51, 61
relationships with books 85
resources: community 6, 9; distribution of 4, 72, 97; economic 1, 33; home 9, 12, 36, 40, 72, 86, 90–1, 103; intangible 9, 12, 87; material 1, 9, 12, 71, 85, 87, 92, 98; online 29, 82; organisation of resources 74, 85; resources and achievement 3; school 4, 27, 40, 71, 85; utilisation of 41, 63, 75, 83, 86, 100
risk society 48

school reading 27, 33, 34, 61, 63
school reading programmes 6, 23, 27, 38–44, 75, 83, 87, 90, 94–9, 101
school/schooling 3, 10, 51, 69; culture 74, 77, 90, 92, 96, 99; design & organisation of schools 27, 69–70; elite schools 18, 21, 56, 80, 85; government schools 1, 18, 21–3; international schools 4, 99
Singapore: context 3, 15–18, 33, 37, 46, 48–50, 62, 86, 90, 97–8, 103; education system/schooling 13, 43, 47, 62–4, 69, 94–5, 100, 102; English curriculum 6, 50–1; English Language Institute of Singapore (ELIS) 49; Integrated Programme (IP) 17, 21, 51; New Education Scheme (NES) 17; policy 16–17, 68, 87, 99–100; Primary School Leaving Examination (PSLE) 17–18; Reading and English Acquisition Programme (REAP) 6; Speak Good English Movement 49; Strategies for English Language Learning and Reading (STELLAR) 6
social class: and academic achievement 4, 13; and curriculum 64; and equitable policies 18, 66; and gender 33–4; and identity 89, 91; and language learning 7, 64–5; and library use 9; and power 1; and reading practice 2, 9, 34–5, 90; and stratification 4

socialise into reading 10, 13, 25, 43, 63, 96
social justice 5, 97
social life around books 43, 71, 83, 96
socially situated 2, 4, 11
social mobility 5–6, 11–13, 16, 18, 45–7
social relations 2, 10, 14–15, 66–8, 70, 73–4, 87, 92
social reproduction 11–12, 15–16, 48, 66–8, 88, 100
sociocultural 7, 9, 25, 73
socioeconomic status (SES) 5, 15, 18, 22, 33, 67, 72, 83, 86–7, 91
socio-spatial 14–15, 66–87
Soja, Edward 14, 66–7
space 2, 13–15, 66–87; organisation and design of 2, 14, 68–70, 73–5, 77, 79, 85–8, 93, 98–9; physical 66; shaping of 74; social 70, 82; spatial connection 70; utilisation of 70, 73–7, 82–3, 86
standards 48–9, 63, 90, 92, 100, 102–3
status 10, 12, 34, 48, 52, 60–1, 64, 89, 99
stratification 3, 5, 16–18, 45, 48, 62
structure 10–11, 13, 90–1; constraints 2, 10, 66–7, 90–2; dominant 12; educational 15, 27, 72, 89
structure-as-problem 67, 90, 92, 94, 103
student-as-problem 27, 67, 88, 90, 103
survey 36–8, 40, 74

tactical globalization 47
taste 11, 47, 57–8
teacher-librarian 87, 98–9
texts: canonical 50, 63; fiction 31–2, 35; literary 22, 53–4, 58, 63, 77, 102; narrative 31, 33; non-fiction 31, 35; popular 54, 57–8, 63; varied 33, 39, 42–3, 63, 83, 85, 102
transformation 15, 27, 67, 87–8; social 11–12, 14–15, 68, 71
transnational 46, 101

value: aesthetic 40, 58, 61, 63; and beliefs 1–3, 27; cognitive 63; entertainment 58–9, 61; reading 12, 25, 28–9, 31, 43, 61, 71, 76, 95; social 11, 83–4; symbolic 22, 62, 73, 77, 86; utilitarian/functional 40, 43, 77, 82; values-laden 65, 101

ways of knowing 21, 53
ways of reading: as cultural capital 8–9, 11, 47, 57, 63, 92, 94, 100–2; gendered 34; learn 1, 7, 25; school-sanctioned/tactical 52, 54–5, 60–2
ways of thinking 7, 52, 53, 55–7, 63, 93
"what if" 93–4, 97, 100
working class 4, 7–10, 61, 64